SKILLS *of the* GAME

Basketball

Laszlo Nemeth

The Crowood Press

First published in 2002 by
The Crowood Press Ltd
Ramsbury, Marlborough
Wiltshire SN8 2HR

British Library Cataloguing-in-Publication Data
A catalogue record for this book is available from the British Library.

ISBN 1 86126 478 X

Dedication
Many people miss the opportunity of their life because it appears in
front of them in dirty overalls and poses as work. Thanks to my mother
and to the game itself, and to my coach Ferenc Banki, and to the players
of Hungary, Kuwait, Iceland, UAE and the UK, who made me a coach.

Acknowledgements
Special thanks are also due to: Pete Norton, the photographer who
produced the demo photographs for this publication; all other
photographs were taken by Chris Tofolos and Mansoor Ahmed; Sharon
Inchley and Ronnie Baker for demonstrating the fundamental basketball
drills; Brian Aldred, assistant coach of Sheffield Sharks, for reading
through the text several times and correcting the English; to the players
and coaches who requested this publication and pushed me hard to
complete it.

Designed and edited by Focus Publishing, 11a St Botolph's Road,
Sevenoaks, Kent TN13 3AJ

Printed and bound in Great Britain by J. W. Arrowsmith Ltd

Contents

Foreword

Young players want to know how they can improve their game and coaches want to know how they can be better coaches. I always say, train hard and learn the fundamentals of the game first. This manual is a good starting point to learn the basic skills a player will need to become an adept player. In addition this book provides the tools that a coach can use in training sessions to widen his or her knowledge of the game. As a pro player I am always in the gym, looking for new drills and directions that will improve my game. This manual provides me with the necessary instructions for a vast array of drills for everyone from the novice player to the pro. Remember it's not only about executing the drills – practice, commitment, ability and concentration are needed as well. A player or coach can never stop learning about this game and having this manual is a good reference.

Steve Bucknall,
England Captain

Steve Bucknall is one of England's most famous players, having played over 90 international matches for England. He graduated from North Carolina University before playing for the LA Lakers in the NBA. Steve has played professional basketball in top leagues in Italy, Greece, Germany and England.

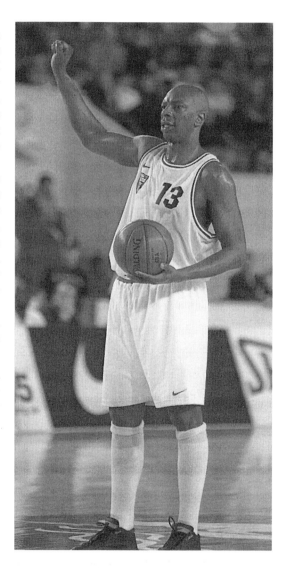

Steve Bucknall, the England skipper, calls an offence.

INTRODUCTION

Basketball from the Street to Arenas

Welcome to basketball! This game is as global as soccer; it is played over the Arctic Circle, in the deserts and anywhere where a small hard flat surface can be found and a basketball board set up. Basketball is a very popular game within everybody's reach, which can be played by young and old and both genders. It is rewarding, fast, pulsing and exciting at every level and wherever its played it is fantastic.

The sport was born in America in 1892 when Dr James Naismith developed basketball in the YMCA of Springfield, Massachusetts, and it spread very quickly all around the world, catching the heart of young people and soon finding its way to the top entertainers of the world. The pinnacle of basketball is the NBA, where most players dream of being, followed by the Olympic Games, the FIBA World Championships, regional championships and international club competitions. It could also be your dream to be in a school team, a local community team or just to go down to an open court and play some pick-up games when the weather permits.

Outdoor basketball is exceptionally popular in North America regardless of whether the area is a suburb or a ghetto. The basketball court and the game itself make everybody equal. It is natural that every player plays to win – the more matches you win the higher advance up the ladder.

This book's intention is to give some help, guidelines and suggestions to those who are just starting the game or already playing regular basketball. It will also give some ideas to athletes and coaches. If you aim to go higher – to be picked by regional teams, country teams, national teams, or prestigious clubs – then you must have a solid grasp of the fundamentals of the game. Basketball is not the kind of game that you can enjoy playing without some mastery of the fundamentals. If you want to progress, you need to hone your skills, and this is what the drills in this book aim to do.

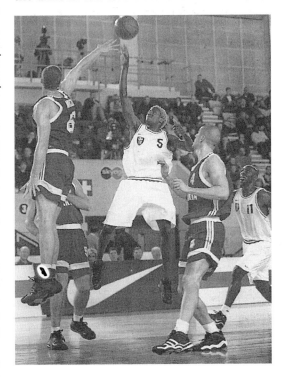

Yorrick Williams airborne.

Steve Hansell flies into enemy airspace.

FACILITY REQUIREMENTS

Basketball is an indoor game despite the fact that in many countries outdoor basketball or street ball, as it's known, is very popular. When it comes to a more competitive level, where teams are well organized and taking part in championships, play is always indoors. If you are a competitive basketball player the ideal and the best floor for to play on is the sprung wooden floor.

TEAMS AND PLAYING TIME

Basketball is always played by two teams, and each team has ten players. In big international events, when teams play a series of games over several days or weeks such as the Olympics, the international governing body, FIBA, allows each team to have 12 players. Out of these ten or 12 only five are allowed on the court at any one time. The game now consists of four ten-minute quarters instead of the previous two 20-minute halves.

It is difficult to say exactly how long a particular basketball game lasts because every time the referee blows the whistle the game clock is stopped. Coaches can take time-out to talk to their team once the clock is stopped but they do not have to use all the time-outs they are permitted.

BASICS OF THE GAME

Object

The main principle is for every team to score as many baskets as they can, preferably more than their opponents. The target is the basket, which hangs 3.05m above the ground. Of course, if your team does not have the ball and so is on defence, your objective is to try to prevent the team with the ball from scoring. Defence is regulated by the basketball rules, which dictate that you are not allowed to deliberately hit, pull or touch your opponent whether they have the ball or not in order physically to prevent him from executing the offensive move. Your defensive target is always the ball and your aim is to stop the opposition setting up scoring situations.

The rule book says basketball is primarily a non-contact sport, but you will soon see that this is only in the rule book. The referee's job is to control the game and penalize any deliberate physical contact, which prevents the offensive player executing his technical movements freely. If the defence or, in some cases, offence, violates this rule the referees will call a foul against the offending player.

Fouls

Every player can commit a maximum of five fouls during the game; when they commit the fifth one they have to leave the court and a substitute will take their place. To record these fouls every player is numbered and the referee gives signals to the scorekeepers to indicate who committed the fouls.

Scoring

Every basket counts as two points, every foul or penalty shot, awarded when a players has been fouled (see above) counts as one point. There is also three-point line 6.25m away from the basket: if you take a shot from behind this line it counts as three points. Therefore, the most important offensive weapon for a team is clearly the shot.

Time Restrictions

There are different kinds of time limits imposed on the players whilst on court. If you look at the diagram of the basketball court you see it is divided by the centre line into offensive and defensive halves. If your team has the basketball the players have to bring it up from the defensive half to the offensive half within eight seconds. This is a new rule brought in to speed up the game; if you fail to do this you will lose control of the basketball and your opponents will be awarded possession. The total offensive time your team has in which to shoot is 24 seconds (including the eight seconds allowed to get the ball into your half); this has been recently reduced from 30 seconds, again to speed up the game. So as soon as your team has the ball it has 24 seconds to complete the offence.

No player can stay in the trapezium-shaped area – often a different colour from the rest of the court – for longer than three seconds. The coaches and players often call this area 'the paint', the 'three-seconds area' or the 'restricted area'.

The Travelling Rule

Basketball's most important rule is the travelling rule. If you, as an offensive player, receive the ball you are not allowed to take more than two steps with it. If you wish to go further you have to start dribbling the basketball; and when you finish dribbling and pick up the ball you may not take extra steps or start to dribble again. You have to take a shot to the basket or pass the ball to one of your team mates. This rule lies at the heart of basketball strategy.

The Start

Every game of basketball starts with a 'jump ball', where the referee holds the ball up in the air between two players in the centre circle. When he releases it, they jump to try to get the ball and tap it towards their team mates.

Team Positions

Basketball, like most team sports, has playing positions such as guards, wings or forwards, centres or pivots. Coaches very often just use numbers to represent the playing positions:

usually nos. 1 and 2 are guards; no. 3 is a wing man or forward; no. 4 is always a powerful forward position and more mobile than the centre, while no. 5 plays mostly under the basket. The rules governing the moves of the different positions and how they train are discussed in Chapter 10.

Unlike other team sports, in basketball there are no restrictions in the movement of players over the court. Guards are normally the smaller players on a team and are usually the quickest. They are responsible for advancing (dribbling) the ball into the opposition's half and coordinating set offensive plays. There are two types of guard: 'point' who is the best dribbler and passer; and 'off' or 'shooting' guard who is a better shooter.

Kelly McHugh controls the ball in traffic.

Forwards or wings are bigger and usually more athletic players, and tend to be the main scorers on teams. Centres or pivots are the tallest players, playing close to the basket, and usually the team's best rebounder.

EQUIPMENT

Basketball is not an expensive sport to play, since all you need is a proper basketball, backboard and rim. Recently, a lot of different kinds of backboards with rims have come on to the market and can be purchased easily.

Clothes

T-shirt and shorts are the most comfortable clothes to play in. It is advisable also to have handy a tracksuit as well or a sweatshirt for putting on before and after matches.

It is vital to have a good pair of basketball shoes. The basketball shoe has recently gone through major developments with regard to ankle support, as this is the part of the athlete's body where ballplayers most often suffer injury, closely followed by the knees. Make sure your shoes offer good ankle support and that right from the start you are familiar with the elementary rules of injury prevention.

WARMING UP

We now have everything that a player needs to start to practise basketball. The game itself and the drills that you go through require a lot of changes of direction, jumps, hard landings and body contacts. Therefore it is important that every time you train or play basketball you are properly warmed up beforehand.

A warm-up could involve jogging, ball-handling exercises or lay-up shooting, and must always be followed by a stretch. After the warm-up and stretch players should gradually increase their execution speed until they can work at full force and full speed.

The most important thing if you want to play basketball is to spend a bit of time, with high level of concentration, on learning the elementary things, because without these you cannot enjoy playing basketball. The best approach is as follows:

Firstly, you have to learn how to **control the basketball** through a series of ball-handling drills. Next you have to learn how to **stop** and **start** because the basketball rules prevent you taking more than two steps if you have the ball in your possession. When you have mastered these two things then you have to think about your team mates, concentrating on **passing** the ball accurately Finally, and most challenging of all you have to learn how to **shoot**.

Learning to stop, start, pass and shoot is the best way to enjoy basketball. Once you have these basic skills under your belt you will be well on the road of becoming a player who is ready and able to take on the world.

KEY

Basketball

Path/movement of player

Offensive player

Pass/path of basketball

Defensive player

Screen

Dribble

Shot

CHAPTER 1
Ball Handling

Before you do anything on a basketball court you must know where the ball is and what you can do with that ball even in the most unusual circumstances. Look at the photographs taken in different basketball games and see what kind of incredible situations can happen – whatever happens, you must still be in charge and able to control the ball. Getting accustomed to the weight, size and above all the speed of the basketball is paramount before we start bouncing the ball around.

Steve Bucknall is aware of where the ball is.

Dribbling has been included among the ball-handling exercises and drills. Dribbling is a very natural skill that most of the players learn without any particular teaching. When you advance to a higher level, coaches will assess your dribbling and how you control the ball in traffic, but we do not need a lot of dribbling, and you therefore have to find a healthy balance between dribbling and other aspects of the game when training. For the purposes of this book, ball-handling drills are nothing other than bouncing the ball around.

BOUNCING THE BALL AROUND

With practice and training you should come to feel that the basketball is almost a part of your body and that you are attached to it. You must know and feel where it is without looking at it, focusing on it, or thinking about it while you are doing something else or moving around – this is the most basic issue if you want to play basketball. You are going to be more successful if you have full control over the ball and try to keep it close to you. You have to protect the ball from the opposing team members who would like to take it away from you, and will make it as difficult as possible to keep the ball and control it. Heavy traffic and physical contact make it hard to retain possession in game circumstances so you have to prepare for the game with ball-handling drills.

The basic practice sequence described below can be very entertaining even for those who have never played basketball before.

Learning to Handle the Ball

1. Throw the ball from your left hand to your right and back first while you are standing, then while walking in the following ways (*see figs 6–7*):

    a. In front of your body
    b. Behind your body
    c. Between your legs

2. Circle the ball around your waist, as fast as you can, clockwise and anti-clockwise (*see figs 8–9*).

3a. Circle the ball around your left leg, then right leg clockwise.

    b. Circle the ball around your left leg five times, then right leg five times clockwise.

c. Move the ball in a figure-of-eight pattern between your legs (*see figs 10–11*). Now try doing it while:

- moving slowly forward
- running
- moving backwards

Fig 8: The circle starts in front of the body.

Fig 6: Throw the ball from left to right...

Fig 9: Move the ball around the body.

Fig 7: ...and back.

Fig 10: Move the ball between the legs...

Fig 11: on a 'figure-of-eight' track.

Now stop for a moment and try some tricks.
4. Put the ball on the top of your head then release it. Catch it quickly behind your body, before hits the ground.
5. Throw the ball up from behind your back and catch it in front of you.
6. Bounce the ball hard on the ground, move underneath it and catch it behind your body (*see figs 12–14*).

Fig 13: Move under the ball and look up.

Fig 12: The ball must hit the ground.

Fig 14: Catch the ball behind your body.

7. Bend your knees, and hold the ball behind your legs with both hands. Throw it forward and catch it in front of you before it hits the floor.

8. Form a V shape with your arms, keep the ball in one hand of the V and let the ball roll across your chest to the other hand and back again (*see figs 15–16*).

Fig 15: The ball starts rolling on your arm...

Fig 16: ...across the chest towards the other palm.

DRIBBLING

Dribbling is the mechanism in basketball for moving whilst in possession of the ball. A player is allowed to bounce the ball using their hand (primarily the fingers, for best control) in a downward motion. The ball is not allowed to come to rest or be 'cupped' in the hand. If this happens a player has stopped their dribble. After ending their dribble a player is not allowed to dribble the ball again until another player touches the ball.

Dribbling is the easiest way to gain space and leave the defender behind, but when you dribble in basketball you are also giving the defence an opportunity to take the ball off you. To retain maximum control over the ball, therefore, it is important to be able to dribble and handle the ball with the same skill and control with either hand, regardless of whether you are left-handed or right-handed, or whether you execute your shots right- or left-handed.

Dribbling Drills

9. Dribble the ball while walking, first with the right hand then with the left hand. Now try it:
   a. with bursts of speed
   b. going backwards

10. Dribble the ball around your body (*see figs 17–20*).

Fig 17: Start the dribble in front...

Fig 18: ...then continue behind, keeping feet still.

Fig 19: Bring the ball around your body...

Fig 20: ...changing hands as you go.

11. Dribble the ball between your legs, on the same satellite track (figure of eight).

Now try building on those drills.

12. Walk forwards, dribbling the ball with your right hand. Suddenly pump the ball hard to the floor, let it bounce high in front of you, run after it and catch it behind your back, bending your knees as you do so.

13. Try the above while moving backwards, but be warned – it is very difficult.

14. Try walking forwards and dribbling again. Pump the ball with your right hand for ten bounces, then bounce the ball between your legs to your other hand. Pump it ten times with your left hand, then bounce it back again between your legs to your right.

> **Dribbling Practice Tips**
>
> - Do not forget to use both hands.
> - Try all the drills, and not just once. Do them every day – make the ball a part of your life.
> - If the first drills were not so easy as you thought, don't be discouraged. Keep trying: you will soon get the hang of it.
> - Do not be put off if other players at the same standard as you do better; just try it again and catch up!

a. Reduce the number of pumps with each hand to five.

b. Reduce the number of pumps to three.

c. Try to bounce it between your legs for every step (*see figs 22–23*).

You did it! Congratulations – you have made progress already. Now stop for a moment and try some more tricks.

15. Throw the ball in front of you, but not too far. Try to create backspin on it so that it bounces back to your hands; you create backspin by holding the ball with your fingers under the ball, rotating your wrists away from your body as you release the ball upwards, so that your fingers point towards your head.

16. Sit down and dribble the ball around you.

17. Sit down and then stand up while dribbling the ball, and without touching the floor with your spare hand. Remember to practise with both hands.

SPEED, STRENGTH AND STAMINA

Do your legs have enough strength? You need strong legs if you want to play this game, to keep you going through the game, to help you speed away from opponents and to cope with strain imposed by constantly having to change direction. You never have much chance to stand still and catch your breath on the basketball court.

Fig 22: Do not look at the ball while dribbling.

Fig 23: Dribble between your feet.

Ronnie Baker dribbles the ball between his feet during a game.

Speed Drill

18. Throw the ball straight up as high as you can. Before it comes down again you must have sat down and stood up (*see figs 24–28*).
    a. Now do it five times in a row without making any mistakes.

Fig 24: Throw the ball up.

Fig 25: Look up at the ball.

Fig 26: Sit down quickly as the ball goes up...

Fig 27: ...and stand up even quicker.

Fig 28: Catch the ball!

Strength Drills

19. Put the basketball between your legs and try to walk to the end of your lane without touching or loosing control of the basketball (*see fig 29*).

Fig 29: Bend your knees, and do not touch the ball while walking.

a. Now try it going backwards.

What about your abdomen? Forget those sit-ups, the basketball can help you here.

20. Sit down on the floor and raise your feet. Hold them together and circle the basketball around your legs 15, then 25, times. Try not to let your legs drop (*see figs 30–31*).

Fig 30: Raise your feet up while sitting.

Fig 31: Circle the ball around the feet.

21. Remain seated and move your legs up and down in a scissors action, trying to move the ball back and forth between your legs. Try this first 15, then 25, times (*see figs 32–33*).

By now you are probably feeling quite tired, but this is a physical game. Drill progression is from easy to more difficult, from simple to complicated. You can do a lot of things with the basketball, some of which are physically demanding. If you have completed this programme, or tried to do it, you will

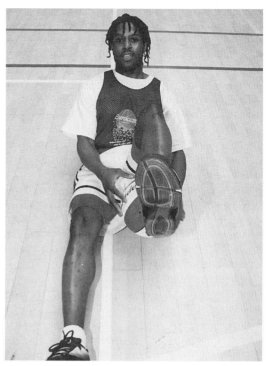

Fig 32: Start scissoring your feet.

Fig 33: Move the ball between the feet.

definitely feel it. Try the drills – some if not all – every day and you will soon notice your fitness and dexterity improve.

The drills above are almost enough for one session, but it is always worth finishing with some repetition. Do you remember the easier drills at the beginning? Repeat two of them, two that you feel you did very well, and then try two that you feel you did poorly. Do you notice any progress? There are coaches out in the street looking for talented people, and you might be one of them, so do not stop bouncing the ball around.

BUILDING ON BASIC BALL SKILLS

Keep in mind the slogan from a great basketball dictator: 'Repetition is the mother of all basketball skills'. So always refer back to the previous practice drills.

The following more complicated drills and tricks can be done without a partner, without a backboard and a rim. All you need is a basketball and determination.

Dribbling

Drill 22

Dribble the ball with your right hand while walking forwards. After five bounces dribble it between your legs and continue straight on, now using your left hand. After another five bounces switch back to the right again.

a. Try the same drill, but now running.
b. Try the same drill, but instead on dribbling the ball between your legs after five bounces, dribble it behind your back.
c. Now combine the two practices. Dribble the ball straight forwards with your right hand. After five bounces, dribble it behind you on to your left

hand, then from your left hand dribble it between your legs back to your right hand. Continue pumping the ball with your right for five bounces and then repeat the drill for a total of five sets of five repetitions.

Drill 23

Dribble the ball straight forwards with your right hand for five bounces. Then dribble it back and forth between your legs and speed up again.

Until now, your dribble was only straight forwards or backwards. Now, after dribbling the ball behind your back or between your legs, change direction too. Move towards your left or right.

  a. Imagine you are in a square or cage 1m across, and dribble the ball as explained above within those imaginary lines, moving forwards and backwards, right and left.

b. Still within the confines of your imaginary square, carry out firstly a one-minute dribbling series, then a two-minute series. Between the series have a one minute's rest practising a simple ball-handling trick from the earlier drills.

Drill 24

Throw the ball up high, slightly in front of you. Run six or seven quick steps, jump up as high as you can, grab the ball with both hands and pull it down close to your body. Then start to dribble, stop and repeat (*see figs 34–36*).

  a. Now when you start the dribble the ball after the grab, dribble the ball behind your back or between your legs, as instructed in the drills above and change direction too. Remember to practise moving to both left and right.

  b. Throw the ball up high but backwards,

Fig 34: Grab the ball high with two hands.

Fig 35: Start to dribble once the ball has landed.

Fig 36: Dribble full speed ahead.

then turn around quickly on the spot, do the same drills as before.

c. Throw the ball up high and forwards and run six or seven quick steps as before. Then jump up as high as you can but do not grab the ball; instead tap it up again before you land. Then jump up again and grab the basketball and start dribble after landing. This is difficult but try it several times, jumping as high as you can each time.

By this stage you should be familiar with the basketball and able to handle it with growing confidence. Repeating the drills will become steadily easier. Can you imagine how far you may go with years of regular practices? Very far, as everything is possible if you do not quit practising (*see figs 37–38*).

Practising with a Partner

Basketball is a team sport, and you have been practising with the basketball alone long enough. With a partner you can introduce more variety into your training sessions, improve your ball-handling skills and get used to working with other players. You still do not need a basketball board.

Start by repeating some of the earlier drills with the help of your partner. Pay special attention to the first and fundamental passing drills.

Spinning the Ball

As a little break, try spinning the ball on your fingers. This has little to do with the game, but it is fun and your friends and family will be filled with admiration; but do not try it in your living room where there is expensive chinaware or in front of a mirror. But be warned: this takes a lot of practice.

Hold the basketball in your palm, with your fingers pointing forwards, away from your body. Close your hand around the ball, so that your index finger moves from a horizontal position to a vertical one, almost pointing towards your nose. Spin the ball, closing all your fingers except the index finger. Keep all your fingers under the ball, as they act as a shock absorber when the ball lands on it. The ball will spin longer if it rests on your fingernail.

If you can keep it on your finger, you can try some variations:

- 'Walk' the spinning ball to your other hand's index finger and back again.
- Toss the ball to make it spin faster and longer with the other hand.
- Is there an ignition key around, or a pencil, or an umbrella? You can put the spinning ball on the edge of these items, and toss!
- If the ball is spinning fast, bounce it to your lower arm and than back to your finger, or bounce it on to your knee and back to your finger.
- After the hard work mastering this trick, it can be used as a way to relax between drills when you are tired.

Fig 37: Wow, I did it!

Fig 38: I am in control.

Drill 25
Stand close to and facing your partner. Your partner raises his arms and you circle the ball around his waist (*see fig 39*) in a figure-of-eight pattern. Once you have mastered this try some variations.

    a. Move the ball behind your back and your partner's back to make an 'O' shape.

    b. Bend your knees and circle the ball around your partner's feet.

    c. Circle the ball around your partner's feet once then around yours once.

After a minute on the drills, change roles.

Drill 26
Use the same drill as above but now start moving forwards, slowly at first, whilst your partner moves backwards. Increase the speed as your confidence in handling the ball increases.

Drill 27
Open your legs and roll the ball towards your partner. Your partner should bend his knees and stop the ball by putting both hands on the ball, with his two thumbs pointing towards each other but not touching. He

Fig 39: The ball moves around the partner's body, too.

straightens his knees, picks the ball up and brings it to his chest, before passing it back to you. Catch the ball and repeat this fundamental passing drill several times. It is important that you do not change or slide your hand on the ball surface from catch until release. Switch roles and repeat several more times (*see figs 40–44*).

Fig 40: Roll the ball towards your partner.

Fig 41: Get ready to catch the ball.

Fig 42: Put your hands on the ball.

Fig 43: Raise the ball and pass it back.

Fig 44: Your partner will catch the ball.

Have Some Fun

As a fun practice to improve co-ordination, try this with your partner. Throw the ball up above your partner's head. He must keep his hands behind his back and catch the ball. To do this he must bend his knees and move under the ball. Now you have a go!

If this is too easy, try keeping the ball behind you when you throw it to your partner. He must catch it with his hands behind him and pass back again, so the ball moves from back to back.

Now face each other, open the feet, hold the ball in front of you, and pass it forwards between your legs.

Fig 45: Get ready to pass the ball.

Fig 47: ...and pass the ball at the same time.

Fig 46: Step forward...

Drill 28

Now exchange some quick chest passes. Step forward when you pass the ball and step back when you receive it. The other foot does not move. You are pivoting on this foot(*see figs 45–47*).

    a. Circle the ball around your waist before the pass, dribble behind your back after receiving the pass, dribble between your legs and pass, circle the ball between your feet and pass. Pass the ball more powerfully each time. Do not look at the ball when you are dribbling but at your partner; you must feel where the basketball is.

25

CHAPTER 2

Stopping and Starting

One of the most important rules in basketball is the travelling rule, which distinguishes basketball from any other ball game and can take a little while to get used to. The travelling rule means the player who has the basketball in his hands is under certain restrictions and has to decide whether to start dribbling, pass or stop with the ball. Consequently, how to stop, and, of course, start with the basketball is a major issue in the game. If you want to learn to stop properly you must first be able to do it without the basketball.

In the past coaches developed many different methods to teach players how to stop; the one explained here is simple and effective. The drills call for a gymnastics bench, which is very common in every indoor sports hall, and are best done in a group with a coach.

STOP DRILLS

Getting the Rhythm

Drill 1
Stepping down off a bench gives you the one-two rhythm that is so important for stopping. Stand on the bench and step down with the left foot. Then bring the right foot down and stop, with your knees bent and your right foot slightly in front of your left. At a signal from the coach, step up again and repeat. After several repeats change feet so that you step down first with your right foot (*see figs 49–51*).

Andy Betts, England's young star, stops with the ball.

Fig 49: Step down from the bench.

Fig 51: Stop rock solid on the ground.

Fig 50: Bring your other foot down.

Drill 2
When you are playing ball you also have to stop backwards. Repeat the above drill now stepping backwards, first with the left foot – one-two – then with the right – one-two *(see figs 52–53)*.

Drill 3
Now stand on the bench with a basketball in your hand. Drop the ball just in front of you to the floor and after one bounce catch it while stepping down from the bench. When the coach gives you the signal step back on the bench and repeat. Start by using your left foot first, then the right.

Stop Drills with a Partner

Drill 4
Once you have acquired a feel for the move you can start practising with a partner. Your

Fig 52: The backward stop; left foot down first...

Fig 54: Step down as the ball is flying towards you.

Fig 53: ...followed by the right.

partner stands on the floor facing you and he has the basketball. He passes the ball to you, but you must step down from the bench before it reaches you – left, right, one-two – and then catch the ball and pass it back to your partner. Step back on to the bench and repeat the process, both with your left foot and right foot leading, until you feel comfortable with the drill (*see figs 54–55*).

Drill 5
Now try doing it backwards. When your partner throws the ball step down backwards, left foot, right foot. Repeat several times, then change feet.

Drill 6
Turn the bench upside down and stand to the outside of it. When your partner passes the ball to you, step towards it over the bench, receive it and stop left, right; then pass the ball back to him and step back outside the bench. Repeat the exercise several times and try doing the same

Fig 55: Catch the ball and stop on the ground.

Fig 56: Turn the bench upside down...

thing but backwards. If you have done all the drills so far, you should start feeling it in your muscles now (*see figs 56–57*).

Drill 7
For this drill you need two benches parallel to each other. You stand on one of the benches while your partner stands on the floor between the benches with the basketball in his hand. Your partner passes the ball to you and you step down and stop – one-two – to receive it as in the earlier drills. Your partner meanwhile steps up on to the other bench facing you. You now pass the ball to your partner, who mirrors your moves and now also steps down and receives the ball and stops. Meanwhile you are back on top of your bench and the drill can be repeated. This exercise should be done at speed.

Drill 8
Now turn both benches upside down. You and your partner face each other, you standing between the two benches, and your

Fig 57: ...and repeat: catch – stop.

partner outside them. You start with the basketball and pass it to your partner. He steps over the bench, receives the ball and stops still with the now familiar one-two rhythm. Meanwhile you step backwards so that you are outside the two benches. Your partner now passes the ball to you, then steps back over his bench, while you step forward over your bench to receive it.

    a. This drill can be played with many variations, and of course you can do it backwards too. Both players start standing inside the benches, but have

to step backwards and stop outside the bench nearest to them to catch the ball, and then step back in once they have passed it.

    b. As another variation, the players can stand so that one always receives the ball inside the benches, stopping with the one-two. The other player always receives the ball outside the benches. The passing can be speeded up so that it is not just only a fundamental stop drill but becomes a very physical, almost conditioning, drill as well (*see fig 58*).

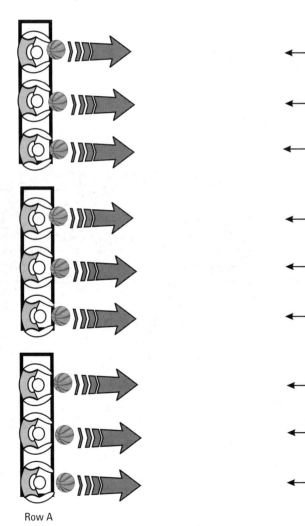

Row A   Row B

Fig 58: The whole team performs the exercise. Partners face each other while standing on top of the benches.

PIVOTING

Once you have stopped with the basketball, you will become the focus of the defence's attention. You will find that the player who is guarding you, or even two defenders, will try to get the ball from you. One way to protect the ball other than just by holding it tightly is by pivoting. Pivoting is nothing more than turning away from our opponent while still abiding by the travelling rule.

It is easy to adapt the stopping drills to learn pivoting. If you step down from the bench with the usual one-two, your second foot become the pivot foot as it touches the floor. You are free to move the pivot foot while your other foot – the one that was first to hit the ground – must remain stationary. By moving your pivot foot, you can do different kinds of turns, fakes and feints, and then you can pass back the ball or start dribbling.

Pivoting Drills

Drill 9
Stand on the bench and drop the ball on to the floor. Step down, left foot first then right, and catch the ball. Once you have the ball in your hands, move your pivot foot to do a quarter turn, then pivot back to your original position. At a signal from the coach step back on the bench and repeat the drill (*see figs 59–60*).

You can also adapt the stopping drills to practise pivoting with a partner. The coach decides how big the pivot step should be and in what direction.

BUILDING ON YOUR STOPPING SKILLS

Drill 10
Now you are ready to remove the benches. Initially, imagine that you are still standing

Fig 59: Rock solid stop, left-right.

Fig 60: Right foot pivots.

on the bench ready to do the one-two stop. Firstly, do it from walking without a basketball, then drop the basketball in front of you, walk underneath it and catch it and stop. Then practise with a partner as you did before with the benches. Once you have got into the rhythm of it, do it backwards also because that is also an important part of the training.

Drill 11
Once you are feeling confident doing these drills, you can start adding pivoting moves.

Drill 12
You have to be able to stop from every direction, stepping across in front of you, stepping across behind you, with your feet placed at different angles. Therefore practise stopping in all directions, firstly without the basketball then with it, until your footwork is secure and stopping firmly becomes second nature. Start by walking, then running, and finally go to full speed.

If you want to do the start properly you must be absolutely sure that you can stop rock solid with the proper balance and you remain in control of the ball. Your basketball skills should build naturally one of top of the other like the chapters in this book. Now that you can stop properly, you can think about starting.

STARTING

Now you have learned how to stop in basketball the next major issue is how to start properly. Fake and start is very often a violation if not executed properly and all too often the referees call a travelling violation against an offensive player. You must know how to start properly to keep on the good side of the referee.

OPPOSITE: A good start gives huge advantage to Delme Herimenn.

We have covered how to stop and pivot. When you are ready to move off again the most important thing is to put the ball to the floor. No matter what direction you want to start in (forward, diagonal, maybe even backwards) the first thing that happens after the stop is that the ball hits the floor. This raises another question about protection and how to control the ball in traffic. Remember that the first priority in basketball is handling the ball – you must always know where the ball is and be able to control it without looking at it, and this is especially vital in starting. Look back at the ball-handling drills covered in Chapter 1 to refresh your memory. You must be able to asses the situation confronting you regardless of whether it is a simple drill in the practice hall or a complicated tactical problem to solve right after the start.

Building on Stopping Skills

The most logical way to practise is to build on the drills learnt during stop training.

Drill 1
This fundamental drill contains two stops, one start and a dribble. Arrange two benches facing each other; you stand on one bench, your part-

---

Practising on your Own

Once you are confident stopping and starting, you can then take the benches away and execute the drills on the open floor and under coach supervision. The drills can also be done without a coach, and you do not really need a basketball board and rim. You can practise alone or with a partner; outdoors or in a very small gym, not necessarily on an international-size basketball court. The important thing is that you get the fundamentals these drills help you learn firmly under your belt. If you do not, you will later on find yourself committing a lot of travelling violations, and numerous referee calls will go against you. This usually has severe consequences not only for your own game, but also the team's overall performance.

Fig 62: Right foot moves first.

Fig 64: Start complete.

Fig 63: Ball goes down to the floor.

ner faces you on the other. You start with the ball. Drop the ball and step down: left, right and stop. When you decide to start moving forwards, step forward with the pivoting leg (in this case the right leg). Put the basketball down to the floor for one dribble and then use the same one-two stop rhythm you used when stepping down from the bench. Then pass the ball to your partner, who now does the same you just did. Ideally you should be able to execute the whole drill without looking at the ground or the ball, but focusing on your partner (*see figs 62–64*).

Go through all the drills described in Chapter 2, adding a 'start' move each time. Make sure you practise starting in different directions – forwards, left, right, backwards, diagonally backwards a little to the left and then slightly to the right. Start off with just one dribble, and then add additional dribbles as your confidence grows; finally, you should be able to dribble the ball freely before passing it to your partner. Go through all the routines of the stop drills first and then add the start as an additional part.

To recap: by now you have sufficiently honed ball-handling skills to know always where the ball is, you can stop properly and you can start.

The next chapter deals with an important aspect of the game, which links players to each other: the pass.

CHAPTER 3
Passing

The turnover – either a violation or loss of possession by the team in control of the ball – is the nightmare of every coach. The most common turnover is the bad pass which misses the team mate, but offensive fault, travelling violation, and technical fault by the referee are considered as turnover too. 95 per cent of turnovers are from bad passing.

The turnover may destroy the whole team's performance. It undermines team spirit and has a negative psychological effect on everybody. It is especially devastating when a team is on a fast break. Statistics show that in most cases of turnovers, 85 per cent of the resulting offences end in a score.

On individual player evaluation sheets coaches often give a turnover –4 points, the largest possible penalty. Conversely, think how much the best passer, the leading player in assists, is rewarded and loved by the crowd. He is the person in the arena who may spot the opportunity that nobody else is able to see, and not only reads the situation correctly, but also executes the necessary moves smoothly and ensures an easy lay-up.

Passing is a fundamental element of the game: effective fast breaks, good in-and-out play, or a nice dish-out after penetration all depend on good passing. The question is how passing can be improved in a sport where athleticism has taken over and the speed of the game has so significantly increased. One answer has to be effective drills.

TYPES OF PASS

The most elementary pass in basketball is the **chest pass**. The pass is best learnt through drills, but when it comes to a game situation, it can be very difficult to execute a basic chest pass while the defence is applying intensive pressure in its efforts to win the ball. Still, it is important to master this elementary pass before you learn other passes.

Steve Bucknall passes the ball to the post.

In the modern game the defence comes very close to us, so when we play a set organized offence we very often use the **overhead pass**. For this pass, hold the ball over your head and try to pass the ball high above the reach of the defence. The defence will try to close down the passing angles so a sound tactic is to do a pass fake above your head so the defenders' hands automatically go up ready to intercept the ball, leaving the sides of their body open. You can then nip in with either a **bounce pass** or a **one-hand pass** to your left or right side. To do a bounce pass you simply bounce the ball on the floor once in the direction of your team mate rather than throwing it straight through the air. This is a very useful pass when you need to circumvent tall players or when defensive hands are guarding the airspace in front of you. Coaches teach and train defensive players to keep their hands up, primarily to prevent shooting but also to deflect or disturb passes and close down space.

The natural reaction of the defensive players when you are trying to pass the ball is to keep their hands up to try to close the upper passing lane. You should always be aware of this defensive reaction; and if you fake a pass with the ball do not then pass it in the same line as the fake. In the worst case you will lose the basketball, but at the least it is likely that your pass will be deflected. Do a bounce pass if you fake up, or pass to the left if you fake to the right. Or you can do two fakes, one up and down, before deciding where to pass. Whatever you do, do not forget that the defence will react to your fake move and close that lane down: do not try to force the ball through enemy hands.

If you take a rebound and you see your team mate far ahead at the other end of the court you can use the **baseball pass** or **javelin pass**, which is a one-handed pass down the court.

When a team goes through the transition moment, that is, from defence to offence,

that is the opportunity for a fast break. During a fast break passing is doubly important. Avoid passing the ball to a stationary player, but try to pass it to a team mate who, like you, is running at full speed. With defensive players retreating or trying to catch up all around you, you have to make the right decision about where and how to pass the ball.

PASSING DRILLS

When you think about passing, selecting the right pass for the circumstances is the crucial issue. You always have to allow for the presence of the defensive players, whose main aim is to prevent you from doing whatever you are trying to do, be it dribbling, passing or shooting. Good passing is not possible without proper ball handling, and can only be achieved through practice, speed and rapid decision making. While you practise passing you have to be able to look around you and see other things happening on the court. The series of drills below help you to do this.

Merely standing facing your partner and practising the basic passes is not the solution, apart from with beginners. Since you have now reached a certain skill level, we need to create something more like a game situation, which forces you to think while moving.

The set of passing practice drills given below is very effective at all levels. It is not boring, and endlessly adaptable, so any coach can develop the drills further as required. The drill can last for about 20 to 45 minutes, depending on the session's main topic. At club level it is a good idea to use passing drills at least three times a week.

Build-Up Drills

Before you put out the poles and cones out, start with some passing drills just on the court. A selection of build-up drills are included here. It is important to tackle these drills with intense concentration and the right speed for the circumstances – rather than just charge along as fast as possible. Speed without accuracy does not achieve much.

Drill 1

Line up in pairs parallel to the sidelines with one basketball per pair. Do simple chest passes to each other whilst jogging.
   a. Now switch to a bounce pass.
   b. Now alternate – one chest pass, one bounce pass.

Drill 2

Exchange simple chest passes while jogging from sideline to sideline. Always maintain the same distance from your partner. Refer to court side A on Fig 66.
   a. Now switch to a bounce pass.
   b. Now alternate – one chest pass, one bounce pass.

Drill 3

Increase and decrease the distance between you and your partner as you move from side-line to sideline. Again, start with simple chest passes. When you are both are at the sideline, you might use a baseball pass to each other. Look at court side B in Fig 66.
   a. Now switch to a bounce pass.
   b. Now alternate – one chest pass, one bounce pass.

Drill 4

Receive the ball on the left side of your body, pass it through the air with your right hand. Look at court side A in Fig 67.
   a. Now try it the other way round.

Drill 5

Increase and decrease the distance between you and your partner as you move from side-line to sideline. Passes are in the air. When you are both are at the sideline, you might use baseball pass to each other. Look at court side B in Fig 67.

Drill 6

Now repeat the drill with the overhead pass, keep the same distance between you and your partner.

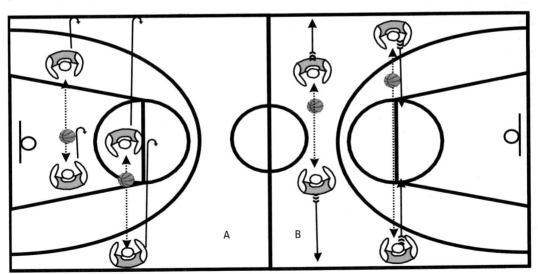

Fig 66: You may keep the distance (A), or increase and decrease the distance between partners (B) while passing.

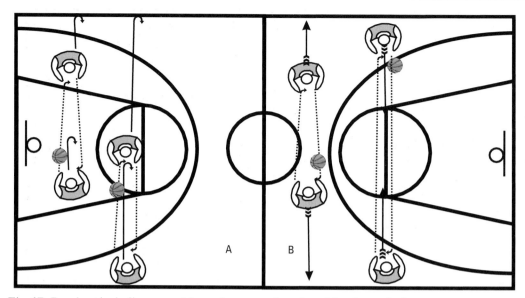

Fig 67: Receive the ball on one side and pass on the other side of your body.

Steve Bucknall looks for an overhead pass.

Drill 7

Coaches can arrange that at a given signal the type of pass and the movement change.

If the movement is too difficult, one option is for one player to remain stationary while the other one moves. When he arrives back you change roles. Bear in mind, however, that you do have to be able to catch and pass the ball while moving backwards, regardless of the pass used.

Passes have to be quick and powerful. If you lose the ball you must recover it and continue the drill.

Now everybody has their own ball. Repeat the seven drills above, with all their variations, two basketballs. This will give you 28 passing drills. Even if you spend only a minute on each one, if you do them all you will have spent nearly a whole half hour only on passing *(see fig 69)*.

Drill 8

With two basketballs, we can restrict the movement of the basketballs, for example ball A must always touch the floor, so a bounce pass must be used to pass it, while ball B is not allowed to touch the floor at all.

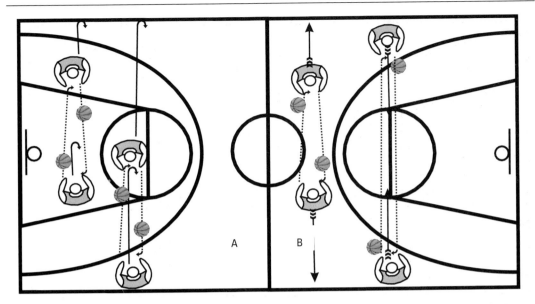

Fig 69: You can work with two basketballs.

It is easier for the players if you can use different colour basketballs. When the coach blows his whistle, the basketballs change roles, so the rules applied to ball A will now apply to ball B and vice versa. One of the players in each pair can be instructed to do only a bounce or air pass. Initially, practise the passes while stationary.

    a. Now start moving from sideline to sideline, keeping the same distance between you and your partner.

    b. Increase and decrease the distance between you and your partner.

    c. Change roles with your partner at a particular spot on the court, for example the three-point lane.

Drills with Poles

In basketball you cannot just stand and do everything on one spot. You have two steps to complete while the ball is in your hands. Within this limited time you have to make a decision about where and how to pass the basketball. The next series of drills will force you to run and practise decision making and precise execution. The poles are marks on the court which constrain the space you have within which to execute your pass.

This trains you in the skills needed to build up an offence later, and, even more crucially, a fast break.

Equipment
The ideal tools are traffic cones with a plastic pipe plugged in the top. The pipe should be about 10–12cm in diameter and 220cm in height, which is almost equal to the tallest players the senior teams have. You will need ten of these. You may use other materials like wood, for example, but bear in mind the pole will often be hit by the ball, and so will need to be stood up and repositioned (*see figs 70–71*).

It is highly recommended that every run should end with a lay-up shot, but the passes can be practised even without a basket at the end. Sometimes small teams do not have access to a floor with baskets for whatever reason, but can still run this training session.

Fig 70: Pass between the poles.

Fig 71: Avoid hitting the poles with the ball regardless of whether you are standing or moving.

Basic Rules

When a pole is hit, this represents a 'turnover' and the player responsible has to stand it up again.

In the case of an error such as losing the ball, hitting the pole or missing each other, the players quit the court and move back to the base line to give room for the next ones.

Coaches should always start with the easiest routine and build up towards the more complicated ones. Change the drill a bit when players begin to do it automatically. Always force them to think – no player is allowed to switch off.

All the drills can be varies by:

• changing roles between drills
• changing roles at halfway up the court while moving
• Using different types of passes (*see figs 72–73*).

Drill 9

You and your partner pass the ball to each other once between every pole. Passes cannot be higher than the height of the pole itself (220cm). Keep a constant distance away from the poles all the way down the court till the lay-up. Remember you have to run, not slide! Try to score at the end (*see fig 74*).

Fig 72: The one hand pass.

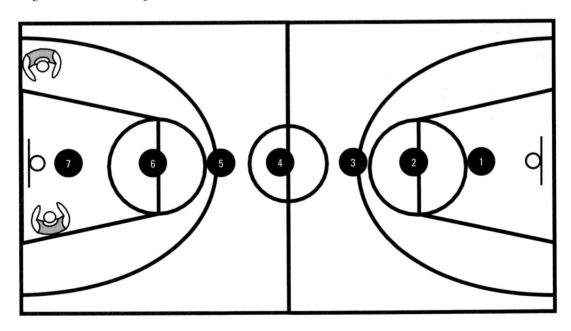

Fig 73: Seven poles are placed on the court as obstacles.

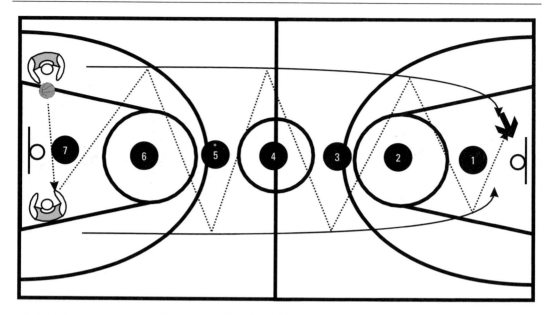

Fig 74: You must pass once between each pole while running.

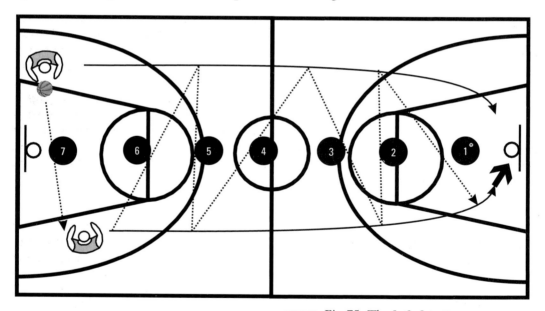

Drill 10

Now complete two passes without hitting the pole or turning the ball over. Complete two passes before pole 7, pass once between 6 and 7 and twice between 6 and 5 without hitting the pole or turning the ball over. Continue to the end of the line of poles.

ABOVE: *Fig 75: The 1–0–1 pattern.*

Drill 11

Complete two passes before pole 7, no pass between 6 and 7, and two between 6 and 5 without hitting the pole or turning the ball over. Continue to the end of the line of poles (*see fig 75*).

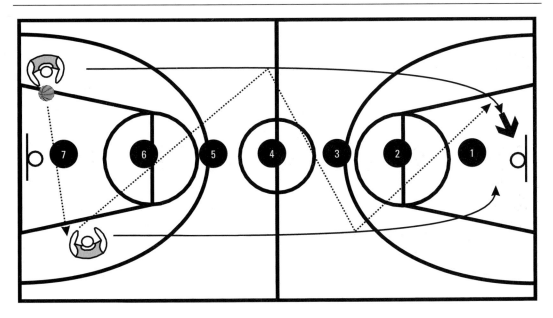

Fig 76: The high speed 1–0–1–0–1–0–1 pattern.

Drill 12

Follow the pattern – one pass, no pass, one pass, no pass, which means: one pass before pole 7, no pass between 6 and 7, one pass between 5 and 6 and so on. No dribbling allowed (*see fig 76*).

Drill 13

Now try one pass, two pass, no pass, which means: one pass before pole 7, two passes between 6 and 7, no pass between 5 and 6, one pass between 4 and 5 and so on.

Drill 14

The next sequence is one pass, no pass, two pass, which means: one pass before pole 7, no pass between 6 and 7, two passes between 5 and 6, one pass between 4 and 5 and so on.

Adding Defence

Drill 15

Now put a defensive player between poles 3 and 4. The defender's movement is limited to one step to right and left. Exchange passes with your partner as before, doing one pass between every pole, including 3 and 4. If the defence intercepts the ball, or you or your partner (the offence) turn over you both step out and move back to the baseline to the end of the queue. Passes can not be higher than the height of the pole itself. Keep a constant distance from the poles all the way down till the lay-up. Remember you have to run, no sliding or dribbling. Score at the end (*see fig 77*).

Drill 16

Now put a defensive player between poles 3 and 4 and between 5 and 6. Again defensive movement is limited to one step to right and left. The offence plays as above, with one pass between every pole, including 3 and 4 and 5 and 6. Keep a constant distance from the poles all the way down till the lay-up. Score at the end.

Grade 1: You may miss one of the two defensive players by one dribble but must pass through the other.

Grade 2: You have to pass through both defenders.

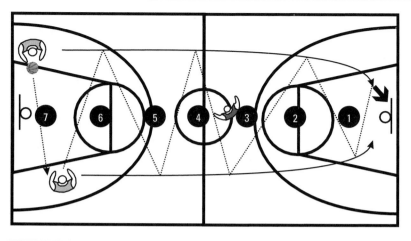

Fig 77: One
defender positioned
between pole
numbers 3 and 4.

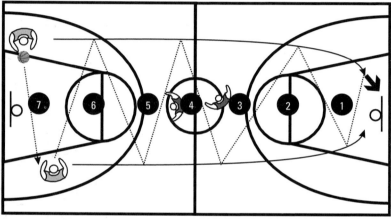

Fig 78: Increase
the difficulty by
adding one more
defender.

If the defence intercepts the ball, or offence turns over you step out and move back to the baseline to join the end of the queue.

Drill 17
Now move the defensive players to stand between poles 3 and 4 and 4 and 5. Defensive movement is limited to one step to right and left. The offence pass the ball to each other as before – one pass between every pole including 3 and 4 and 4 and 5.

Grade 1: You may miss one of the two defensive players by one dribble but must pass through the other.

Grade 2: You have to pass through both defenders.

Grade 3: Add a third defensive player.

If the defence intercepts the ball, or offence turns over you step out and move back to the baseline to join the end of the queue (*see fig 78*).

Drill 18
You and your partner now have a ball each. Exchange passes between every pole. One player always passes in front of the pole the other behind the pole. You have various passing options:

• both do a bounce pass
• both do an air pass
• one of you always bounces the other passes at the air

Fig 79: Now we use two basketballs. One player for each.

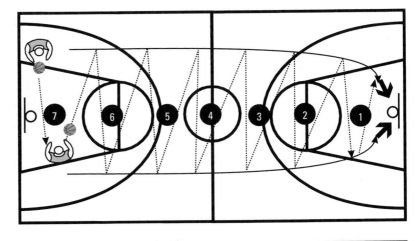

Fig 80: In this example, we changed the positions of the poles on the court.

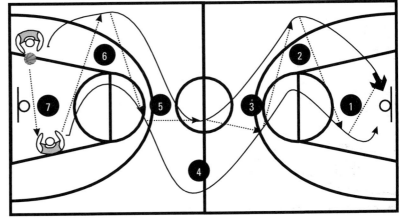

You can change roles halfway up the court.

You can repeat most of the earlier drills (9 to 14) except those where we had defence, with two balls (*see fig 79*).

Now change the position of the poles on the court (*see fig 80*) and run the same set of drills through again.

- You and your partner exchange one pass between every pole.

- You have to adjust your running speed each time.
- Passes cannot be higher than the height of the pole itself.

All previous drills including the drill with defensive player(s) can be done with the cones in this configuration.

CHAPTER 4

Shooting

We have been working continuously on stopping, starting and passing, but to the forefront of most players' minds is the most important thing – scoring! It is a good idea to have a coach around you when you first start learning how to execute a shot, but an experienced player could also give you advice and correct the errors that occur most frequently during shooting. You can always do some of the drills in this chapter, which are the first steps towards building up a stable and well-controlled shot.

TYPES OF SHOT

When you look at the different type of shot, the first, and most basic, is the **lay-up shot**, which is executed by taking two steps, jumping up in the air, elbows under the basketball, and using the backboard to score. A lay-up from the right side of the basket should be completed using your right hand and from the left side using your left hand. The jump into the air on the left side is from right foot, and from the right side is from the left foot. This is the most important and elementary shot in basketball.

The next shot to learn is the **jump shot**, where a player jumps up into the air from a stationary position and executes a shot from mid-range or long-range distance. In the modern game the jump shot is not always used, especially when players are shooting from downtown or far from the basket, when the **spot-up shot** is more suitable. Here the emphasis is on shooting very quickly once you receive the ball rather than on the jump into the air.

We also have the **hook shot**, which is executed close to the basket inside the paint or in the low-post area. This shot is released far away from your body with your shoulder and elbow keeping the hook shot away from the defender. The game has seen

John Amaechi, England NBA player (Utah Jazz), takes a shot.

a sharp decline in the use of the classic hook shot because defence has greatly improved; the traffic is now so dense inside the paint that there is not enough space to execute a classic hook shot, and short defenders can steal the ball easily while you execute it. However, it is usually still taught because it is a fundamental part of the game. What players now execute much more inside the paint is the **baby hook**, a shortened version of the classic hook shot. It is executed by jumping into the air from both feet, keeping the ball close to the body and shooting it up high quickly.

An important new type of shot is the **turnaround jumper**, an athletic shot in which the shooter starts the shoot with their back to the basket and completes a 180-degree turn in mid-air before the ball is released. This is normally done by tall players, but very often forwards too: because the defence comes in ever closer in the modern game, you have to be extremely good at jumping to try it. The turnaround jumper is often combined with the **fade-away**, when after the turnaround the shooter does not just jump up into the air to execute the shot but jumps backwards away from the defenders hand and body. This type of shot requires a little extra power so that the ball reaches the basket.

Finally, there is the **foul shot**, covered in Chapter 2.

In European-style basketball, in particular, players are very good at spotting each other on the court and shooting from long range.

Many teams in Europe do well because their shooting ability is so good it can make up for any lack of athletic ability.

The constant battle between defence and offence means that you often have to shoot when you are tired, which requires more physical power in order to compensate for lack of precision. A simple, clear and undisturbed lay-up shot rarely happens in a close game, except maybe when a ball is stolen from the point guard or a long, clear baseball pass on a fast break finds an open player.

BASIC SHOOTING DRILLS

Technique

Drill 1
1. Stand facing your partner with your legs apart in a comfortable stance, one foot slightly ahead of the other.
2. Your partner adopts the same position and rolls the ball towards you *(see fig 81)*.
3. Stop the ball by bending your knees and putting both hands on the ball, with your thumbs pointing towards each other but not touching.
4. Extend your knees and pick the ball up close to, but not touching, your body.

Fig 81: Catch the ball on the floor.

Fig 82: Raise the ball above your face.

Fig 83: Shoot the ball to your partner.

5. Raise the ball above your head, up in front of your face so that it lies in your right palm (or left palm if you are left-handed). The other hand provides support. You must be able see the target under the ball.
6. Extend your arm upwards to start the shooting action, aiming at the back of the ring and keeping your shooting hand behind the ball (*see figs 82–83*).

Drill 2
You receive a simple chest pass from your partner, and shoot the ball back into his raised hands.

Drill 3
Increase and decrease the distance between you while you and your partner are shooting the ball to each other. Do not increase the distance so far that it would be physically difficult to execute the shot. Look at the arch of your shot and how the ball behaves.

Drill 4
Most good shooters have a reverse spin after the ball has left their hands: the flicking action of the fingertips as the ball is released ensures the ball is given some backspin. Do you have this? To check, take the ball into your hand and shoot it up. Let it bounce on the ground in front of you, about 2–3m away from you. Does it bounce towards you? If it does, you have a good reverse spin!

Drill 5
Are you unsure of your shooting technique? Lie down on the ground and shoot the ball up. Every time just concentrate on co-ordinating the arms. Bring the elbow under the ball. Think about the reverse spin. All shots finish at the fingers – imagine you are waving the ball good bye at the end (*see figs 84–86*).

When you are at home you could practise the shooting action in front of the mirror several times, without the ball of course.

Senior players sometimes have individual shooting styles, which may be different from the ideal shooting techniques outlined in books and articles, but before you can develop your own style you have to master the basic skills. Shooting is a precise skill, requiring intense concentration. The focus of that concentration is the basket. The good shooter is focused on the basket, even when dribbling, passing, screening and other offensive activities are taking place. If a player always keeps the target in his mind during offence, his shot selection will improve as well. Scoring is the most attractive part of the game, but despite this it is important to learn other aspects of the game, like stopping, starting and passing first. If you are comfortable with those elements of the basketball game, you will be more confident shooting.

Fig 84: Lie down on the floor.

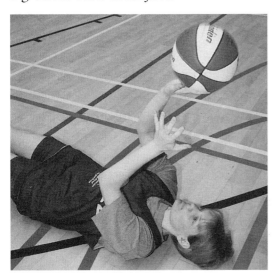

Fig 85: Shoot the ball up into the air.

Fig 86: Extend your arm and add spin to the ball.

Focusing

Swish! That is the sound you want to hear when the ball goes through the net without touching the rim itself. This is the favourite sound of the guards and forwards. Since the three-point shot entered the international game, the value of reliable outside shooters has rocketed.

Thames Valley women can shoot as well as anybody!

Steve Hansell takes an outside jump shot.

Drill 6

1. Move under the basketball board, and step to the right or left side of it, at an angle of about 45 degrees between the baseline and the rim. Do not go right under the board, but do not move too far at the beginning.
2. Put the basketball down on the ground right in front of your shoes.
3. Open your legs, put one foot slightly ahead of the other, bend your knees and put both hands on the ball. Your thumbs should be pointing towards each other but not touching.
4. Extend your knees and pick up the ball close to, but not touching, your body.
5. Raise the ball above your head, up in front of your face so that it lies in your right palm (or left palm if you are left-handed).

The other hand provides support. You must be able see the target under the ball. The target at this first stage is the quadrangle painted on the board. You must shoot the basketball to the higher corner of the quadrangle.

6. As you start the shot itself, extend the arm upwards, and keep the shooting hand behind the basketball.

7. Catch the ball and put it down again, and then repeat the shot many times (*see figs 89–90*).

Variation a. Stay in the same position and carry out the same shooting action, but now your partner rolls the ball to you on the ground after a basket or rebound. Take ten shots and then change roles.

Variation b. Do the same, but now your partner uses a chest pass to pass you the ball.

Drill 7
Now move further back, first one step, then two. Still use the backboard for the shot.

Drill 8
Increase and decrease the distance from the basket now. Never shoot from the same spot twice, but move only on the imaginary 45-degree diagonal. Try one shot from close in, then from other a step behind, then return to the first spot. Forget about the three-point lane when you are learning how to shoot.

Drill 9
Go close again, and switch the target from the backboard to the basket itself. Shoot the ball directly into the basket.

Drill 10
Now try to score without the ball touching the rim.

Fig 89: Roll the ball towards the shooter.

Fig 90: Now, shoot to the basket!

Drill 11

Move to the other side and repeat the set of drills. You should stay within your range but can shoot now from other angles too. Change roles with your partner after ten shots. Remember to compete – either with yourself or with your partner. After a shot, when your partner has scooped up the ball and passed it to you, pass the ball back to him with a chest or bounce pass and move to another shooting spot.

The shooting target is not the rim itself. Coaches differ on where exactly to focus when shooting. The most common choice is the centre of the ring. However, it has been shown through recording statistics during a game that 84 per cent of missed shots were short, and in the case of three-point shots this number was higher still. Furthermore, if the shot was short, 85 per cent of the total rebounds went to the defensive team but if the shot was long only 40 per cent of the rebounds did.

The lesson is clear. Instead of focusing on the centre point of the basket, players should try to target the far side of the rim. They will find their percentages increase, especially on long-range and three-point shooting; the most remarkable improvement is in three-point shooting. Focusing on the far side of the rim can greatly improve team and individual shooting percentages and reduce the risk of turning the ball over to the opposition.

In game circumstances, cardio-respiratory strain affects a player's muscular control and body awareness. The effect is different for every player, depending on the pressure of the game. Muscular control lessens as the heat of the game intensifies. A move itself is practised many thousands of times and stored in the cells of the nervous system. However, the *execution* can be different. A player must consciously adapt how he shoots his shot – adding a little extra power to shoot longer.

If you have a close look at a basketball rim on the ground, you can see how large a target it actually is – large enough to fit two basketballs through it at once; try it and see.

Some coaches advocate using the backboard whenever possible, but there is no particular advantage in this. The important thing is the long shot. If you had the added burden of always having to think about the backboard when shooting, it is quite possible that your long-range and three-point percentages would decline, and experimenting with this might be harmful to the team's achievement.

A team's success depends on its shooting percentage. If a team's players are shorter than most of their opponents, it is crucial that they can produce results from the floor.

Look how John Amaechi does it in the game.

Silus Cheung shoots from 'downtown'.

PLANNING YOUR SHOOTING TRAINING

Shooting drills include other basketball skills, such as passing, cutting, rebounding. These must be practised with the same level of concentration as the shot itself. After one shot and before the next one athletes should not switch off mentally, but concentrate executing the linking moves accurately.

Targeting

As a rule of thumb, use the backboards for:

- lay-ups
- power moves
- close jump shots

Aim at the rim for:

- turnaround jumpers
- free throw
- hook shot
- long-range shot
- three-point shot

Chris Haslem uses the backboard for a lay-up.

Andy Betts puts up into the rim.

How many minutes in a training session are actually spent shooting depends on the preparation time available. During the season, it is advisable to have shooting in every practice: less immediately after a match, then more and more as the date of the next game approaches. It often happens that the last session before a game contains 60–70 minutes of shooting practice out of the 90-minute total floor time.

What kind of drills are included in the practice plan depends on two things:

- How many baskets are available in the gym?
- How many players are present at the particular session?

Where facilities are far from ideal, the coach may also have to take into consideration how many balls he has available.

Shooting and Weightlifting

There are two questions players frequently ask:

- May I lift weight during the season?
- Will the weightlifting mess up my shot and slow me down?

The pros and cons of weightlifting are the subject of many scientific research projects. To analyse such research and go into detail would fill almost another book. In summary, you can lift weights during the season with the following provisos:
- the drills must be specially selected
- they must be custom-made for you

When putting together your weights programme, pay attention to:

- age
- body weight
- number of repetitions
- number of series

- weight applied
- intensity or speed

If you ignore any of these rules, your shot may be adversely affected. Weightlifting will certainly mess up your shot if it is infrequent and ill planned. Occasional bursts of 'iron pumping' will only cause problems, especially during the season.

Finally, here is a quote about every basketball player's idol, Michael Jordan.

> Jordan added a new wrinkle to his routine this season. He lifted weights virtually the entire season, even during the finals ... 'I never lifted weights before because I was always afraid it would negatively affect my shot ... Obviously it did neither. I feel a lot stronger now.'

Interview from *USA Today*, 15 June 1992.

ADVANCED COACHING DRILLS

You must be competitive during shooting practice. Coaches can motivate their players by announcing the individual or team results loudly to everybody. Almost every drill has a time limit, and the players must know in advance what are excellent, good, medium, and poor scores within that particular time. They compete with themselves, too, always aiming to beat their previous best. This is particularly important for those players who are a bit behind the others, so they can measure their own improvement. If an outstanding score is achieved by any player, praise his performance in front of the others.

During shooting drills, players must be constantly reminded to 'gear up' to game-like speed. Intensity is the most crucial factor when you only have limited floor time. There is no doubt that every kind of shooting drill is beneficial – the vital question is, which are most *effective*?

Timing

Coaches: get a watch with a timer function. You can then follow the work in progress and swing around all the basketball boards without having to keep your eye constantly on the clock. The timer will beep when the pre-set period expires, and this indicates that the actual drill is over.

Every time the player moves for a shot from the right side of the court to the left he must stop in right-left foot order. From the opposite side of the court he stops in left-right foot order. The jump stop is not allowed.

Before describing the drills themselves, here are the various shooting options with which they are constructed. The final combinations can be incorporated into every drill. The instructions relate to the shot execution.

Steve Bucknall's speed counteracts the larger size of the defender.

Shooting Drill Options

1. Straight shot
2. Shot after fake shot (secondary shot)

Options 3 to 5 can all end with either a straight shot or a secondary shot.

3. Stop and fake, step across with the pivot foot in the direction from which you came, do one dribble and shoot.

   Variation a. Do more dribbles (up to a maximum of three) and shoot.
   Variation b. After one dribble, reverse and shoot.

4. Stop and fake, continue the move and shoot after one dribble.

   Variation a. Do more dribbles (up to a maximum of three) and shoot.
   Variation b. Do one dribble, reverse and shoot.

5. Receive the ball, continue with one dribble, without stop, and fake shot and shoot

   Variation a. Do more dribbles (up to a maximum of three) and shoot.
   Variation b. Do one dribble, reverse and shoot.

It is not practicable to use all the above combinations together at once. In one training practice you might use some, in others different ones, but this does not go against the principle of 'repetition is the key to success'. The drills are repeated throughout the whole season.

The coach gives the next instruction/direction without stopping the drill itself. The coach should introduce the drills in one practice, and once the players know them, will not interrupt them unnecessarily – only if there is something extremely important to explain.

With two baskets available for a session it is possible to use three to six different drills for team shooting, and four to eight different kinds of shot in each drill. If there are more boards in the gym, you can fit in more shots per person within the same time.

The team shooting drills always contain other basketball skills. The player's move does not begin or end with the shot – he has to dribble, pass, catch the rebound or choose between two options, to cut, or move without the ball. These moves are very important, and coaches should encourage their players to play always as though they were in a real game situation. Before a player arrives at the exact moment of his shot, he must have been involved in other tactical and technical elements of the offence.

The next question is: do you practice shooting with or without defence? The answer is both. Shooting without defence gives the player and coach the opportunity to correct the form and technique of the shot. On the other hand, when we do include defence in the practice, there is little point having the defence play at only 75 per cent intensity or less, as some coaches do. It is better to create situations that favour the offensive player and requires 100 per cent from the defence. Success in these drills is a special credit to the defence, but to score is almost compulsory for the offensive player.

Team Shooting Drills

The following basic rules apply throughout.

• The two main baskets available in the gym are used throughout.
• A time limit is given for each drill
• A minimum and maximum guideline is given for the number of players taking part. If there are more than this limit then the number of shots per minute will decline and the drill becomes less

effective. Players have to stand off the court too long waiting for the next shot.

Never forget the slogan of teams with limited training resources: use every second to repeat something.

Drill 12

This drill requires two players and one basketball.

1. Player B starts the move into the court. Player A passes the ball to him and runs towards the first basket on the court.
2. B receives the ball from A and executes a jump shot. After the shot A runs towards the middle of the court.
3. B goes for the rebound and passes the ball to A.
4. B moves towards the next basket, receives the pass from A and takes the jumper. At this stage, when A and B are at the second basket on the court, C and D starts the drill on the same path (see fig 96).

• Players A and B go around the court taking shots at each basket.
• Do the drill five minutes clockwise and five minutes anticlockwise.
• The coach will pay attention to how the passes are made, and the intensity of the run.

Drill 13

This is a good drill when you have more than 16 players at the session. We now have six passers on the court, each one passing to one basket.
1. Player A starts the drill. He passes the ball to the first player and receives the ball back.
2. C takes a jump shot, follows his shot, takes the rebound and passes to the second player.
3. C receives the ball back, executes the shot and carries on as before.

RIGHT: *Fig 96: Shoot at all baskets in the gym.*

4. C moves around the court taking shots to each basket.
5. B starts the drill when C takes his jumper at the second basket (*see fig 97*).

• Change the passers every two minutes.
• Change the direction of travel.
• Change the kind of shot.

Drill 14

Who scores first? Players A and B start together at two side baskets. Both of them must score two baskets on their side before they can drive to the main board at the other end of the court. The winner is the player whose ball goes through the basket first at the main basket. If either of them misses the shots at one of the side baskets, he must stay and repeat the shot till he scores. The coach can ask for a lay-up or a jump shot (*see fig 99*).

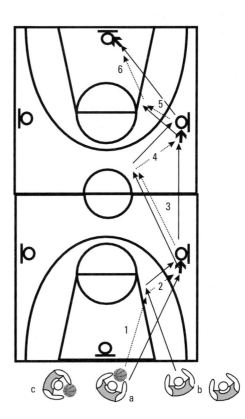

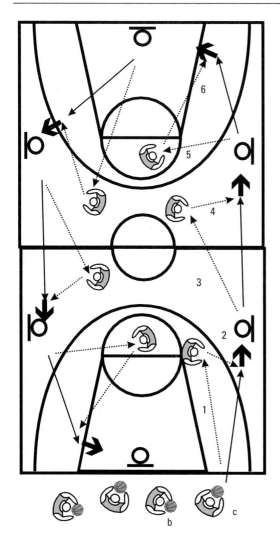

Fig 97: Use passers at each basket.

Steve Bucknall completes the lay-up.

Drill 15
Players: 6–10. Time: 6 minutes

1. Player B passes the ball to player A.
2. B cuts to the elbow, receives the pass back from A and takes a jump shot. 3. B follows his shot, rebounds it and goes to the opposite corner.
4. A now turns to D and repeats the whole drill to the other side, and so on (*see fig 100*).

- Change the passer (A) every two minutes. This drill is a good passing workout for player A. He must do one or two quick steps to the side of the player he is working with.
- Everybody must follow his own shot.
- Players should not touch anybody else's rebounds.
- Dribble after rebounds and then pass like an outlet for a fast break.

- After receiving the ball, a player can penetrate for different kinds of lay-ups.
- The coach calls the next passer from those who have just followed a shot; the drill does not need to stop to change passers.
- Always look around you at what is happening on the court – do not be a robot!

Drill 16
Players: 6–10. Time: 6–8 minutes
You need at least four balls for this drill.

Fig 100: The point team shooting drill.

Players A and B and E and F have a basketball each, players C and D do not.

1. Player D starts the drill by cutting towards A and receiving the pass.
2. D takes a jump shot, follows it, rebounds, passes to C and goes to the end of the line.
3. A repeats the movements of D to the other side and the drill continues so all the players have a shot (*see fig 101*).

- Dribble after rebounds and then pass like an outlet.
- If there are only six participants one side must pass the ball after rebounding while the other keeps the ball.
- For this drill you must change the distance of the shots. Start from close range and move away gradually.
- The coach must demand very high levels of concentration on all moves. All players must be on constant alert.

Drill 17
Players: 7–11. Time: 2 × 5 minutes
All players have a ball except player G.

Fig 99: Lay-up competition using the whole court.

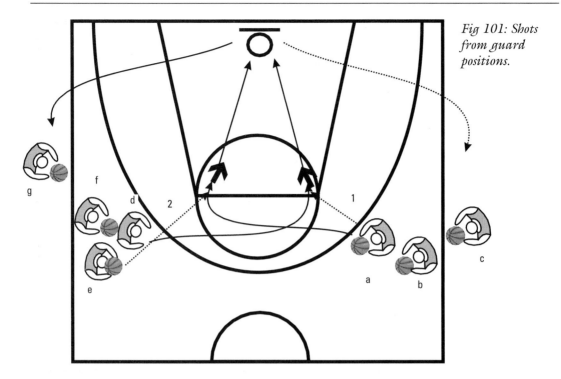

Fig 101: Shots from guard positions.

1. Player D starts by passing his ball to G and cuts to the other side.
2. D receives another ball from A, drives down to the low post position and stops.
3. A, after the pass, cuts to the other side and receives the ball from G.
4. A takes a jump shot, follows, rebounds it, and drives to the end of the line. 5. G pops out, receives the ball from D, takes a jump shot and rebounds his own shot.
6. D moves up to the key and is ready to receive a ball from E (*see fig 102*).
- A player always shoots with a different ball from the one he started with.
- Quick passes and cuts are required.
- Players must see the whole court.
- This is a very intensive drill. You must follow the rebound, pass to the right person, and move to the right place.
- The dribble, pass and cuts must be game-like.
- Change sides after everybody has had a turn.

Drill 18
Players: 6–12. Time: 6–10 minutes
    Players G and F have basketballs under the basket. A, B, C and D are in a line without a ball. E stands under the basket, ready to rebound.
1. A starts by cutting towards the corner.
2. He receives the ball from G and takes a jump shot.
3. G goes to the end of the line.
4. E rebounds and waits to pass, replacing G.
5. A goes under the basket to rebound, replacing E.
6. F passes the ball to B (*see fig 103*).
- This is a good team drill if you only have a few balls.
- The drill is very intensive.
- All players must run back to the half court, or put a pole or marker on the court somewhere to indicate where they have to go back to.
- The drill can be done across the court, parallel with the sidelines from baseline towards the free throw lane or the other way round.

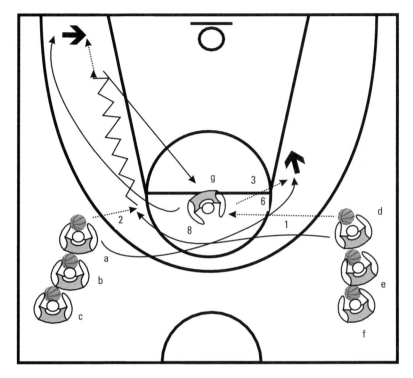

Fig 102: Pass-cut-
dribble complex
shooting drill.

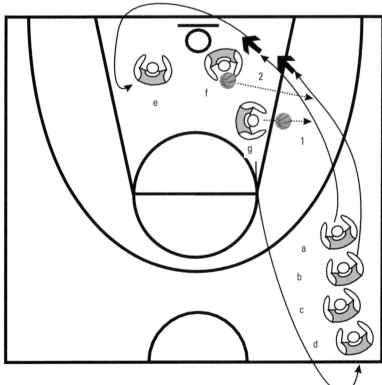

Fig 103: Team
shooting drill with
two basketballs only.

- Bad rebounding can disrupt the drill, so the coach must emphasize the importance of precise rebounding.
- If this is the last drill of the session, set targets – for example, practice is over if 10, 15 or more shots are made in a row. If anybody misses the shot the count starts again.

Drill 19
Players: 7. Time: 6 minutes
  Two players work together.
1. D passes the ball to G and cuts to the corner on the same side of the floor.
2. G passes the ball back to D and turns towards A.
3. A passes the ball to G, cuts to the corner on the same side and receives the pass back.
4. D has been dribbling the ball during this time while looking at what is happening between G and A on the court.
5. After passing to A, G turns again to D. D passes the ball to G, cuts to receive the ball

back and takes a jump shot (*see fig 104*).

- This is another drill that requires a high level of concentration.
- The coach must substitute the passer at least every two minutes.
- The movement of the players is only partially restricted to certain areas of the court. Where they move after dribbling for the shot is up to the individual.
- When a player is dribbling while his partner is passing, the dribbler must look at what is happening on the court.
- The oncoming two players must be alert as well, and not hit G, who is passing the ball to the shooters.
- If everybody has a ball, they should bounce them while waiting for their turn in the drill.

Drill 20
Players: 5. Time: 1 minute per round

1. Player B passes the ball to C, cuts to the

Fig 104: Action, game-like shooting drill.

*Fig 105: 5 players–
5 minutes shooting
drill.*

corner, receives the pass back from C and takes a jump shot.

2. A passes the ball to C and cuts to the elbow, receives the pass back from C and takes a jump shot.

3. D repeats the movement of B on the opposite side of the court.

4. E repeats the movements of A on the opposite side of the court.

5. Everyone rebounds his own shot and goes back to the starting place.

6. Everybody moves round one position clockwise after one minute (*see fig 105*).

• Five players are the ideal number for this shooting drill, but the coach can include extras – for example, two players following each other from certain spots.

• Each round of shooting lasts for one minute only.

• The most important rule is that no player is allowed to touch any other's rebound.

• If you miss the shot, the penalty is to chase after the rebound no matter how far away it has bounced, and still be back at your place in time.

• The passer must always keep the shooting order, and the shooters must be alert not to accidentally hit the passing guard with two balls at the same time.

A coach can always create his own team shooting drills from particular parts of his team to practise man-to-man or zone offence. It also helps the offensive tactical repetitions.

If the coach has an assistant they can split duties: the assistant can conduct the team shooting drills, while the head coach is doing something else at the other end of the court. This division is very useful if their are many players in the session.

Drill 21 – The 3 × 2 Minute Shooting Test
Players: any even number. Time: 3 × 2 minutes
   Players work in pairs

1. Player A shoots for two minutes from close range (blue line). Player B gathers up the ball after each shot and passes it back to A.
2. After the two minutes are over, B takes his turn.
3. A shoots again, this time from medium range: within the three-point lane but outside the restricted area (green line).
4. After the two minutes are over, B takes his turn.
5. A now shoots three-pointers only (red line).
6. After the two minutes are over, B takes his turn (*see fig 106*).
• The rebounder's role is vital. Without his dedicated co-operation the shooter's result could drop significantly.
• If it is well organized, this can be a very effective high-intensity shooting drill. In 12–14 minutes both players will have executed about 100–110 shots, fast and in competitive spirit.

Evaluation of results:

	Excellent	Good	Poor
Close range	32 or more	22 or more	18 or less
Medium range	25 or more	20 or more	15 or less
Three-pointer	20 or more	16 or more	12 or less

Drill 22 – The Seven-Point Triangle Shooting Test
Time: 2 minutes

Grade 1: The spots are numbered on the court, and a player is allowed to

Fig 106: 3 × 2 minutes shooting drill.

move to the next shooting spot only if he scored. If the shooter miss the shot he must return to spot no. 1 and start again, no matter from which spot he missed the shot. If he completes the test within two minutes, he must start again (*see fig 107*).

Grade 2: A similar system applies, but now the player must score twice in a row before he moves to the next spot. If he misses a shot he must go back to the starting point, no matter from which spot he misses, or whether it was his first or second shot.

Evaluation of results:

	Excellent	**Good**	**Poor**
Grade 1	3 complete rounds	2 complete rounds	less than 1 complete round
Grade 2	2 complete rounds	1 complete rounds	less than 1 complete round

Drill 23 – Hit the Three-Pointer
Time: 2 minutes

Grade 1: This drill is set up like Drill 22 one with the following variations:

- A player who hits the three can take one step to the next shooting spot. If he miss the three-point shot, he must step within the three-point lane to receive the ball from his partner, and shoot from medium range.
- If he hits the medium range shot he can go back to take the three-pointer from the same place from where he missed it before. If he misses the medium-range shot, he must do a lay-up, than move back to the three-point lane for the next attempt.
- If the shooter miss the three-pointer, the medium-range, and the lay-up as well, he is obliged to go one spot backward for the next three-pointer (*see fig 108*).

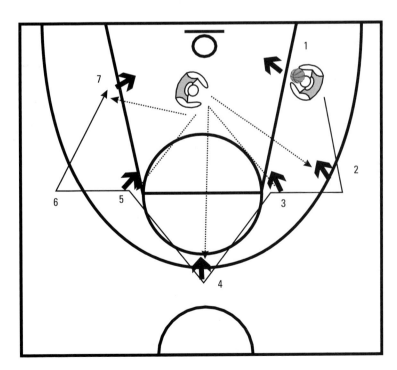

Fig 107: The seven point triangle shooting test.

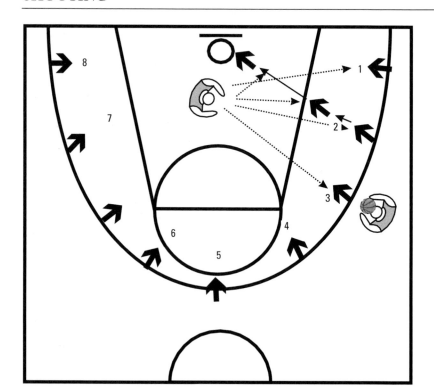

Fig 108: Hit the 3s.

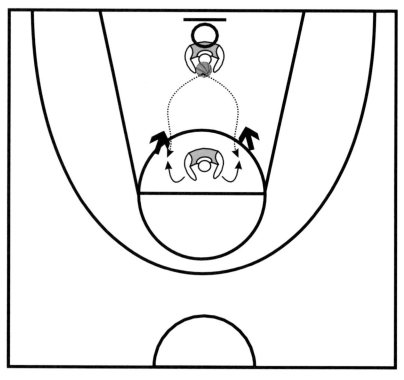

Fig 109: Turnaround jumpers.

Evaluation of results:

	Excellent	Good	Poor
In each round	20 three-pointers	15 three-pointers	10 or fewer three-pointers

Drill 24 – The Turnaround Jumper
Time: 2 minutes

This drill helps to practise this rather difficult form of the jump shot.

1. The shooter stands with his back to the basket.
2. The passer – who is rebounding as well – drops the ball at the shooter's left or right side.
3. The shooter must notice the ball, without looking over his shoulder, step towards it and execute a turnaround jumper. If the ball is dropped to the left he starts the move with his left leg, if to the right he starts the move with his right leg. He must catch the ball after one bounce. Practise first within close range, then extend the distance (*see fig 109*).

Attention Players!

If you are practising on your own:

- You may significantly increase the number of shots taken.
- If you put a hard-surfaced board as a ramp under the basket, the ball will come back to you when you have made the shot.

Evaluation of results:

Excellent	Good	Poor
20 hits or more	18 hits or more	12 hits or less

CHAPTER 5

Rebounding

If you hear about a player's overall statistics, the second figure after the scored points is how many rebounds he had per game, regardless of which position he was playing. Of course you are expecting many more rebounds from a big man (pivot) than from the point guard, but if the point guard or off guard can help in rebounding, this is exceptionally valuable to basketball coaches. In the NBA, rebounding specialists are very highly priced and some of them are just selected for that particular role; coaches and managers are then happy if he scores only six points, say, but leads in rebounds within the team.

Phrases like 'rebounding machines' and 'dominating man at the boards' are always very positive, and many players like to hear them, especially if their offensive skills are not exceptionally good and they are not capable of scoring more than 20 or 30 points in a game. Many such players balance such low scoring statistics with more than ten rebounds per game.

What actually is rebounding? Rebound happens after a failed shot: if the shot goes in the ball goes to the other team and they must take the ball out of bounce under their own basket. Rebound is a transition point. If you look at the tactical point of view of the game, the moment that we call rebounding – when the ball is gathered up after a shot – is the closing moment of the defence and the starting point of the offence, and as such is a very important element of both aspects of the game – defence and offence.

What are the main features of the rebounder? Most people would put 'good at jumping' at the top of the list. If you jump higher you can get more balls, so if you have a good vertical leap you have natural advantage; however, not all high jumpers are good rebounders. Positioning and upper body strength are also important qualities in a good rebounder. On top of this, a rebounder has to be able to secure the ball when he gets it. It is not enough just to touch the ball, the rebounder has to control it, and – usually in heavy, physical traffic – secure that ball for his team. The biggest priority is how to score from the rebound in the quickest possible way.

If we look at the positioning, what is the goal? To be in an ideal position to get the rebound, of course. However, if you stand right under the rim, you have to jump out to get the rebound, and while you are in the air, especially if you are jumping backwards or to the side of the basket, you are easily pushed out. You are off balance and so are less likely to gain control of the ball.

In defensive rebounds the majority of the shots that are missed are short, so defensive rebounding it is not just a matter of a vertical leap, intercepting the ball in the air and then securing it. It starts with the box out, keeping the shooter or player away from the ball. By the same token, if you go for the offensive rebound when you see a shot is released, your prime objective is to get inside position the defender. Then if get the ball, you always have the option of putting it back to the hoop.

Delme Herimenn pulls down a rebound.

To get the rebound it is not very easy in traffic, as the defence has tactical ability and big players are very athletic now, so it may take several jumps and not just one to catch and pull down the ball. Therefore the first jump is very important. The speed of the second jump right after landing from the first jump has become increasingly crucial in getting the vital rebounds. We all know how to work on jumping abilities, how to increase vertical leaps, what kind of methods exist to increase upper body strength, and this section is not about conditioning. It is not about plyometrics and other jumping drills; this chapter is intended to give you some rebounding drills that you might have not come across before.

When thinking about rebounding, never forget the physical aspect of the game: it is war under the boards with players using all available means that the referee and the rules tolerate to secure the ball. Tactics work best if you play to the limit of the written rules or to the limit of the referee's tolerance, and the further you can go without being caught or penalized the more successful you will be. Therefore, players have to be ready for plenty of contact in traffic, respond well to rapidly changing circumstances, and in case of a no call situation, should never give up the fight. Always try to regain position as quickly as possible.

If the defence win the rebound they effectively strip the offensive team of an additional chance to score. If they fail, and so give the opponents one or even two more attempts to shoot within that offence, they really hurt their chances: usually one out of three attempts will definitely succeed. Furthermore, if the offence has control of our board this will boost their confidence enormously, because they are not under the same pressure to score which they would be if they were playing a team that was good under the boards and known for getting the rebounds.

Of course, all this is equally valid if you are in offence. Offence is easier to execute if you are sure that you have excellent rebounders on your side. The majority of the rebounds will get back to you so there is less pressure to get high scoring percentages.

It is therefore not surprising that players with good rebounding statistics are very highly valued on all basketball teams.

The first thing the defensive rebounder has to do is establish body contact with the player he is guarding, then turn around, box him out move towards the ball. If you stop to watch the ball and wonder whether will it go in or not, the offensive player may seize the opportunity to gain the inside position and rebound or tap in the ball successfully, or your reaction time will be too slow and you end up over-compensating and move to an undesirable position like just under the rim.

PRACTISING WITH A BALLOON

Before we play we have to have some drills to practise rebounding thoroughly. To start off, we can make use of a simple children's amusement – a filled air balloon; the balloon must be filled with air, not helium, so it does not fly away and it must be the standard round shape the size of a basketball or slightly bigger.

Basic Rebounding Skills

Drill 1
Stand facing a partner in the central circle or one of the two circles at the far lines. You both have the same objective: to keep the balloon in the air within the circle for 24 seconds without your partner touching it. You can fight each other with any legal basketball means to try to gain possession – you will see this is a very physical and tough drill (*see fig 111*).

Fig 111: Stay inside the circles.

Drill 2

This drill has the same rules as above, but this time two play against two. Each team has to touch the balloon as many times as it can within 24 seconds.

Protecting the Ball

If you rely purely on jumping you might never get the ball. You have to secure the ball, work hard body against body within the limits of the rules. Many players should get credit for keeping good rebounders away from the basket. The next drills are developed with this in mind.

Drill 3

Stand in the middle of the circle while your partner stands at the edge. When the balloon is put in the air, your job is to box out your partner and not let him touch the balloon before it reaches the floor.

The Tap

The tap is a crucial touch where you put the offensive rebound into the basket or simply adjust the path of the ball into the rim. In order to be successful the jump must be timed correctly, and the next drills will develop this skill.

Drill 4

Stand under the basket. Your coach or partner holds the balloon up and releases it, and you must try to tap it into the basket, preferably in less than five jumps (*see fig 112*).

Fig 112: Tap the balloon into the basket.

Fig 113: Tap both balloons into the basket.

Fig 114: Who taps the balloon into the basket?

Drill 5

Stand under the basket again. This time your coach or team mate holds up and then releases two balloons close to the basket and your job is to tap both balloons into the basket before one of them reaches the floor (*see fig 113*).

Drill 6

Stand under the basket with a partner. Your coach holds one balloon above the basket and releases it, and your objective is to tap the balloon into the basket before your partner (*see fig 114*).

Drill 7

Stand under the basket with your partner. This time there are two balloons, one for each of you. When one of you has tapped his balloon into the basket he can go against his partner for the other balloon. Your goal is to try to put both balloons into the basket.

Drill 8

Now four players stand under the basket, two against two. When the coach puts up the balloon in the air each team tries to score first. The restriction is that if once player touches the balloon he cannot go up and touch it a second time; his team mate has to touch it instead.

The Struggle for Position

The fight for the position prior to the shot, especially inside, takes a lot of power and strength. Being inside, closer to the basketball, which will hit the rim, is a natural advantage. Size matters here too, of course, but any player can box out, which means taking the position inside nearer to the basket before our opponent does. This is especially important if you are up against a much taller player. Establishing body contact and taking the inside position, so closing the route towards the basket when the shot is made, are crucial to getting rebounds.

Drill 9
Now for the rough, tough, physical part of the rebounding. This drill involves four players and one ball. One player has the basketball in his hands, standing in the defensive position at the elbow, facing with the shooter. Shooters' partners are at the corner and shoots the ball to the basket and follows the rebound, then the defensive player puts the basketball on his body and tries to box him out and push him away, but only with the basketball. Of course he cannot hit the shooter with the basketball. If the rebound bounces on the floor twice, or in the next version of the drill once, then the defence wins and the players change position. If the player in the offence, the shooter, can take the rebound his job is to do a quick outlet pass, and the next player will dribble to the elbow, while the defensive player does the same job again (*see fig 115*).

Important Points

To execute a successful box-out and rebound:

1. Move towards your opponent
2. Establish body contact
3. Turn around, knowing where your opponent is
4. Take an inside position and prevent him from moving in or towards the basket.
5. Now jump towards the ball, catching it with both hands.
6. Holding it tightly, pull it down close to your chest and secure it
7. Immediately look for an outlet pass.

Drill 10
This is the same as drill 9, except there are now two players facing the shooter, pushing him with the ball and trying to prevent the outlet pass (*see fig 116*).

Drill 11
Now the focus of the drill shifts to being offensive-orientated. Instead of the outlet pass, the rebounder must try to put the

Fig 115: The 'war' under the board.

Fig 116: We increase the number of 'bodies'.

basketball back to the basket, while the defender, with another ball in his hand, still pushes hard against the rebounder.

Drills for Three Players

Drill 12

For this drill player B starts at A's elbow and C is the rebounder.

1. A takes a shot, C goes for the rebound, grabs the ball and puts it back to the basket. If C scores, he gets a point.
2. Next B takes a shot; if he misses the rebounder C goes for the ball, catches it and puts it back. If the shot goes in then that is a point for the shooter, if the shot is missed the rebounder must get the ball before it hits the floor, and that is a point for him.
3. After scoring all players have to leave the ball and concentrate on the next shooter, and can try to disturb the shooter if they wish (*see fig 117*).

Drill 13

This is an offensive rebounding drill. Players A, B and C stand in a row facing the right or left side of the basket.

1. A puts the ball up to the left side of the basket, then turns around and faces his team mate (B), marking the third player (C).
2. B taps the ball back to the backboard then turns right to the opposite way, again marking C.
3. A and B must allow C to grab the rebound. C is not allowed to tap, but after he has the basketball on his hand he must work his way through against the two defenders under the basket.
- We can impose restrictions on the offensive rebounder by stipulating that he must put the ball up within three seconds.
- As variations, C can have one dribble or no dribbles
- If we add a fourth player, perimeter or partner, C can pass the rebound out to the perimeter for an outside shot (*see fig 118*).

Fig 117: Shooter rebounder competition.

Fig 118: Offensive rebounding.

Drill 14

This is a complex box-out rebounding drill. Player A acts as a point guard, B stands on the left, and C on the right side.

1. A passes the ball to C and cuts behind the back of C under the basket, facing towards the middle of the court, and takes a defensive position inside the paint.
2. B moves into the key and receives the ball from C inside the key just above the foul line outside the paint, and faces towards the mid goal.
3. C moves in front of him and B hands over the ball. C plays one against two and tries to score. B's goal is to stop C penetrating and force him to make a contested outside shot, then immediately box C out so he can grab the rebound undisturbed. If this does not work and C ends up in a position where he could penetrate and beat B in a one-on-one situation, A steps up to help B.

4. When C has made the shot then it is A who boxes him out while his team mate grabs the rebound (*see fig 119*).

There are many other ways of teaching and practising rebounding, but the above drills should help you develop your skills. Implement them at your practices as much as you can.

By now it should be clear that it is not always the tallest player, or the highest jumper, who grabs the rebounds. In theory, somebody who is a good, high jumper should automatically be an excellent rebounder. However, because of the constant physical contact, the push and the fight under the basket, other skills also come into play. For a start, you may have to jump up twice for the rebound, so going up into the air again right after landing is important. In extreme cases you may have to jump up for a third time, and then you may only be able to toss or tap the ball somehow, in some direction.

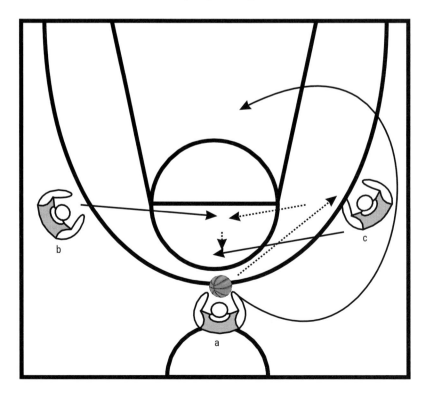

Fig 119: 1 against 2 and box out drill.

This is why balloons are good tools for rebounding drills: as they are relatively slow-moving, they enable you to calculate the position of the object that you are fighting for, namely, the rebound – and also allow you time to give each other hard physical work.

In summary, when rebounding you have to be very physical and a bit like a punch bag in that you must be capable of taking a pounding and still establish a presence and go up for the ball. It is not just a matter of tolerating the physical war under the boards; if you can find just the right amount of aggression tolerated by the rules of the game then you are going to be a great rebounder and rebounders are very highly valued by their coaches and team mates alike.

Defensive Rebounding

Securing and grabbing a rebound is so important for the team in defence because it denies the opposition a second chance at shooting and gives the defence an opportunity for a quick transition and fast break to score an easy basket themselves. Pulling off such a move then naturally increases the team's confidence in their defensive teamwork.

CHAPTER 6

Fast Break, Easy Transition

Easy baskets are the most important points that a team can achieve during a game. They are the most destructive physically and psychologically to the opponents, and if we want to roll over them and run them down then a series of easy baskets are needed.

Basketball's most spectacular moment: Tony Dorsey dunks after a fast break.

What is the best way to achieve easy baskets? The fast break. A good, successful, quick team is probably a good fast-breaking team. Our team must have excellent ball-handling skills, good passing ability where the players are not selfish and can spot each other very well. To make a good fast break the players have to be able to read the situation on court quickly and make decisions accordingly. This skill is not acquired overnight and needs a lot of practice.

The history of basketball shows a lot of teams at every level from NBA down to district level whose major feature is the fast break – run, run, run! So how do you build up a good fast-breaking technique. Of course if you want to play fast you need good cardio-respiratory endurance. The whole team should have this so they can really operate at high speed during the whole game.

The fast break is not an element of basketball that you can really practise alone. Even the simplest version of the fast break requires two players, while the most common fast breaks are with three, four or, if very well organized, five players.

First of all the execution of lay-ups at the end of the fast break is vital. No matter how fast we are running or how much we are moving the most important element of the game is the bucket, namely, the score. If you steal the ball in a game as a result of good defensive effort and have a good chance to score virtually undisturbed, nothing is more embarrassing than missing a lay-up. When we do the four-corner drill below, the most important thing is to execute the lay-up at high speed. Do not miss any of the shots. It is interesting that mistakes happen more frequently as the drill progresses and the players start to tire.

THE FOUR-CORNER DRILL

During the practice the coach changes the set of the four-corner drill; he can change the intensity by adding or taking out basketballs, but the players never stop executing and scoring the lay-ups. This makes it like a game situation, when players on court have to listen to instructions and maybe change the offence according to the instructions coming from the bench.

For example, the coach may pull out the basketball and put it in the circle at half court, asking for a pass to him, so that when the drill is changed there are only two basketballs in action. Once the players have understood the change in the drill then the number of balls can be increased again. This means the transition moments are also pressure moments; for example, after you have just executed your lay-up, you immediately turn to face the court and look at what is happening, which exactly mirrors a game situation.

Roger Huggins finishes the fast break.

Practices must always be game-like and linked to certain aspects of the basketball game. For this we start with the four-corner fast break drill which helps to build up endurance and also demands high level precise execution, This drill does not allow players to turn off even after a score when they have seemingly completed the drill.

The Basic Drill

Diag. 30.
The team is distributed in equal numbers to every corner. One player (A) stands under the basket holding the basketball and waits for the signal from the coach to start. We do the same at the other end of the court (player B), and start from the right as the majority of players are right-handed (*see fig 123*).

1. The players under the basket (A and B) pass the ball to the right to two other players (C and D) who run to receive it.

2. C and D then pass the ball to the other corner at the other end of the floor to E and F.

3. C and D run as quickly as they can to receive the ball back, execute a lay-up and go to the next corner.

4. The passers (E and F) take the rebound and give an outlet pass (*see Glossary*) to the corner and then also moves on to the next corner.

- The principle of this drill is very simple: you always move up one corner round the floor.
- Of course the left side has to be used as well as the right.

Building on the Basic Drill

The coach and his assistant usually stand in the centre circle with some additional basketballs. When the players get into the rotation of the drill and understand the system, the coach increases the number of basketballs in play.

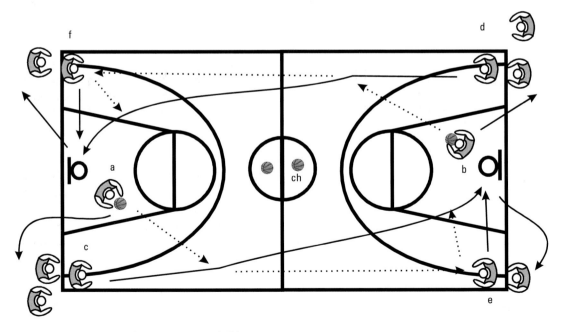

Fig 123: Basic set of the four corner drill.

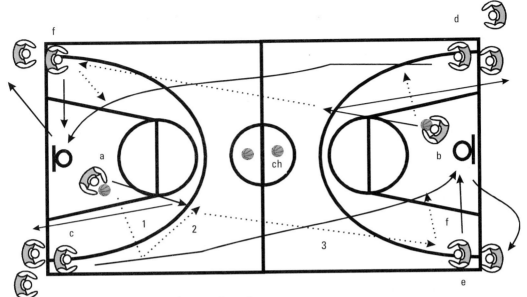

Fig 124: We increase the number of passes.

There will be a minimum of four balls with 12 players, and you can introduce more if there are more players. The whole drill is very intense and requires a high level of concentration and the players have to execute it very precisely.

With this drill, the coach can talk and changes the drill while the players are continuing running and they do not stop, even for a second, to watch for demonstrations. Apart from increasing of the number of basketballs, the coach can also withdraw a ball from the drill by asking the players to pass him a ball, and this reduces the intensity of the drill.

Variation 1

The coach can also ask a particular player, usually one of the bright ones, to change the drill slightly. For example, the rebounders (A and B) now pass the ball through an outlet, follow the fast break and receive the ball back; they then pass it to the opposite corner (to E and F), then go back and get ready to make the next fast break move. The player runs as quickly as possible, receives the ball from the corner, executes a lay-up and then moves onto the next spot (*see fig 124*).

Variation 2

Next we can add another pass, with a player (A) receiving the pass and then again passing to the running player (C), who will continue on to the corner, receive it back and score! (*see fig 125*).

Variation 3

The next move is simple – an outlet pass received back in the middle. The player at the opposite corner moves up to the key, receives and passes down to the runner, who executes a lay-up (*see fig 126*).

Variation 4

Now try an outlet pass, pass back to the middle and then again to the side. The side then passes up to the elbow, cuts, receives the basketball and scores. Of course the rebound is taken by the player who was at the elbow and now immediately turns and continues on the other side of the court. This is a very quick and very intense variation.

Coaches can also change the drill by specifying what type of shot players finish with – maybe a power lay-up first, then a close-

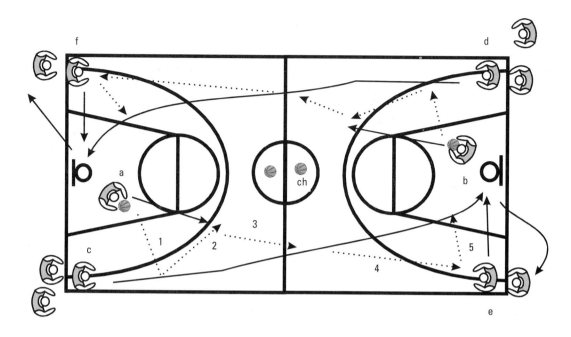

Fig 125: Whoever runs will touch the ball three times in this drill.

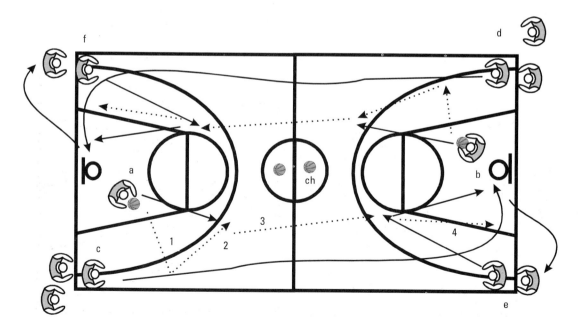

Fig 126: Player flashes at the elbow.

range jump shot and so on. It is always up to the coach to move the drills on, bearing in mind the level of ability of the players.

If you do the four-corner drill with variations it will take about 20–25 minutes, which is great conditioning exercise. The four-corner drill concentrates on one thing only, and that is executing a lay-up, which is achieved by good passing and high speed.

ADDING A DEFENCE

Thus far the players have not had to deal with a defence. However, in a game situation it rarely happens that you are able to drive to the basket without anybody trying to prevent you from scoring. The majority of fast breaks are 2 v. 1, 3 v. 1, 3 v. 2, 4 v. 2 or 4 v. 3 situations.

The next series of drills creates these various scenarios. These drills include virtually all elements of basketball but every drill is slightly weighted in favour of the offence to give the players a real chance to practise their offensive fast break moves.

3 on 1 Drills

Drill 1
This drill is based on the simple three-man weave. The players start on the baseline, and the ball is in the middle (A).

1. A starts by passing the ball either to the left or right (see Fig 127).
2. B and C each touch the ball once then pass it back to A in the middle of the court.
3. A passes it back, to B or C, who are now coming towards him, and takes up the defensive position.
4. This creates a 2 on 1 situation, and when the players reach the other end of the court the two offensive players have to score against the one defender. When they have finished they come back to the sideline (*see fig 127*).

At this stage we are doing the drill just in one direction; the next progression is to execute the same drill, but this time the player who took the shot runs back to the defence and starts a 2 on 1 down to the other end to score.

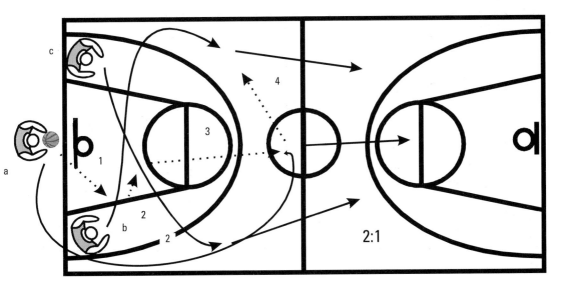

Fig 127: 3 man's wave ends 2:1.

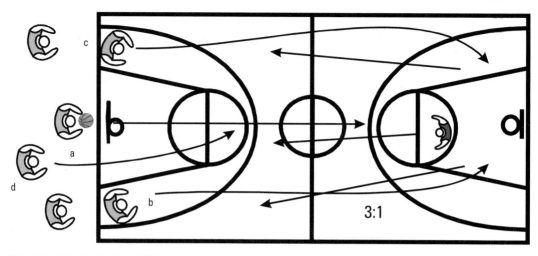

Fig 128: The basic 3:1 drill.

Drill 2

Teams who want to play good fast breaks have to spend a lot of time practising 3 on 1 situations a lot, so the next drills are 3 on 1 drills. The defensive player stands at one end of the court and the three attacking players come up directly for the 3 on 1, not starting from the weave. The offence must score but they have only one shot, with no rebounds, and no possibility to correct: there must be pressure on the shooter because in a 3 on 1 situation you always have to score. If the shooter misses the attempt, he has to stay and play defence against the next coming three. This drill is only done one way each time.

We can now build on this drill. The players go down 3 on 1 to one end of the court and if the shooter misses the shot he will stay in defence as before. If he makes the shot, the offence players have to come back and play a 3 on 1 at the end of the court from where they started, this time with the middleman from the next three playing in defence against them (*see fig 128*).

Drill 3

This 3 on 1 drill works on the same principle as above. Players go down and play 3 on 1 at one end of the court. If the offence miss a shot then the player who missed it stays on defence, while the other three come back up the court and have to score against one player who is standing in the zone or higher. If they miss this 3 on 1 they have to go back again with the same rules and come back again, so they can quit from the offence if they score on the way back. Each time they are allowed only one shot with no rebound. Weaker teams can be allowed to score from a rebound to begin with, but later must also progress towards perfect execution by being restricted to only one shot.

Drill 4

This drill uses a slightly different approach, which requires the players to read the game much better. Players still go one way on the court, but this time you have two defensive players – one at the side of the court and one under the basket. The three offence players have to go through the defensive players and score.

The coach can add further restrictions to the drill by permitting dribbling only in one half of the court:

• No dribbling in the half where the three players start, which forces the players to do more passing. Dribbling is allowed at the offensive end when you come to the 3 on 1 situations.

- Dribbling is allowed while the players build up their offence, but not at the offensive end where the defenders are.

Drill 5

Now try the 3 on 1 drill back and forth. Restrictions can be applied, the most basic one being that if you miss the shot or turn the ball over you go and play defence. This gives the defensive players an incentive to work hard to try to get out of playing defence. Again, restrictions can also be imposed on which parts of the court dribbling is allowed in. This forces the players to think while they are executing the drill.

If the drills start to feel monotonous and the players are going through the moves on auto-pilot, it is essential to change the restrictions immediately to wake the players up again as they have to cope with the change in the drill. This is important because every slightest change gives different signals to the players and the better player can read it faster. Our overall goal is always to improve the ability of the players to accurately read fast break situations. Practise the 3 on 1 fast breaks constantly, as they are almost a game fundamental.

Three on 1 and the 2 on 1 situations happen frequently if there is a sudden steal or a team goes on a fast break after a good rebound and outlet pass. Players in a 3 on 1 situation should wait till the ball is in the middle before taking that crucial decision, that is, whether to carry on towards the basket, take an outside shot or just give a pass to one of the players on either wing.

When we practise the fast break the other major issue that players and the coaches have to bear in mind is that the fast break situation, regardless of how many players are involved, does not exist for long. Therefore we have to create drills where fast breaks

occur like they do in a real game. If you are good enough and if you make the right decisions you can score quickly and easily. If not, you have to work much harder to get the desired basket.

3 on 2 Drills

As a logical step the next scenario is the 3 on 2 drill. To maintain the connection with 3 on 1 drills you have two options.

Drill 6

Firstly, we can put two defenders at one end of the court and have three players go against them, 3 on 2, and try to finish. In this case the offence are allowed to take rebounds to encourage them to follow their shots. When they have finished the offence they simply come back to the sideline. If the shooter misses and the defence takes the rebound, the player who took the rebound leaves the floor and the player who missed the shot turns and stays on defence.

Drill 7

Alternatively, we can combine the 3 on 1 and the 3 on 2. Players run 3 on 1 at one end of the court and finish their offence with only one shot. If they make it, they come back and face two players from the next three and do 3 on 2. If the shooter misses at the end of the 3 on 1, he stays and plays defence (*see fig 129*).

Drill 8

Now we can develop the drill further, so that the offensive team plays 3 on 2 at one end and then on the way back faces another

---

You Need to Know

In the modern game 3 on 1 situations happen roughly twice during a close contest, but knowing how to cope with them is the springboard towards solving and reading more complicated fast break situations.

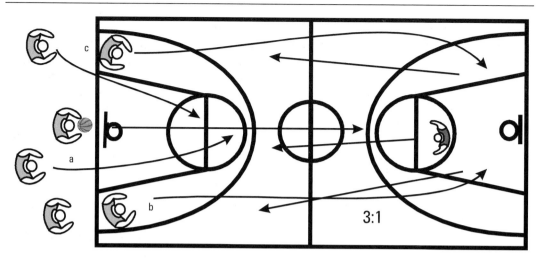

Fig 129: 3:1 followed by a 3:2 drill.

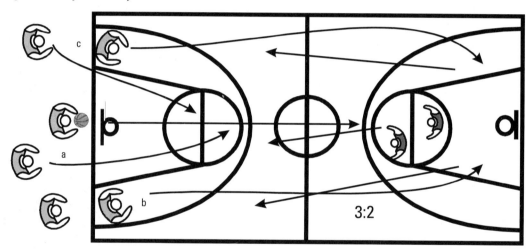

Fig 130: Twice playing 3:2.

3 on 2 at the other end, playing against two players from the next three. The coach can change the restrictions. For example, the players might be allowed only one shot or they may have to follow the rebound. On the way back it might be best to allow only one shot just to secure the continuity of the session. The number of passes can also be restricted and dribbling can be banned in 3 on 2 situations. This, of course, will force the players to look for cuts and locate their team mates (see fig 130).

DRILLS FOR 12 PLAYERS

The ideal number of players in a practice session is 12. With 12 players you can set up four three-member squads, each ideally wearing different-coloured vests. When four teams are playing at once it is a good idea for them to compete and count their score. If there is a foul against the offensive team that could count as a basket. As the 3 on 1 drills are the basis for every fast-break situation, 3 on 1 is a good starting point for a multi-player drill.

Drill 9

Two teams start at one end of the court and two teams at the other.

1. One colour group starts from the left end of the court and goes 3 on 1; the defensive player is one of the three at the other end, whose team mates stand outside the sideline following what happens.
2. When the 3 on 1 finishes, the defensive player picks up the ball, his two fellow players step in from the sideline and they now complete their 3 on 1 offence against one of the players from the other end.

- The usual 3 on 1 restrictions can be applied: that is, only one shot is allowed and the offence have to complete and score from this fast break.
- If the offence fail to score the player who made the mistake or all three players can be penalized. The message to all players must be that in a 3 on 1 situation, a basket is compulsory (*see fig 131*).

Drill 10

Now run the same system with 3 on 2. This is another important element of the game and comes up in many fast break situations. In this scenario you may allow rebounding for the offensive team to reinforce the importance of the offensive rebound. But if you want to concentrate on the accuracy of the execution, then allow only one shot.

Drill 11

Now divide one of the teams up among the others to get three four-member teams. This way you can practise 4 on 2 situations much as you did before with 3 on 1 and 3 on 2. Now two players from one team play defence and two stay on the sideline while another team plays in offence. At 4 on 2 it is best to allow no dribbling at all to encourage quick passing among the offence as they try to find a way to score. Coaches must emphasize how to fill the lane in these situations, as they offer many solutions to the offence (*see fig 132*).

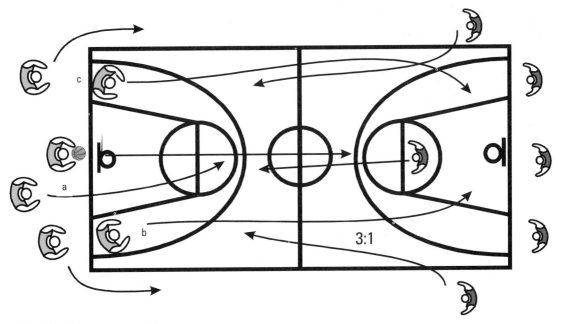

Fig 131: The non-stop 3:1.

When Will It Happen?

Fast breaks can happen at any time and stage of the game. They could come early, at the beginning or towards the end of the game, when of course the importance scoring from them is greatest of all.

Drill 12
Needless to say the next step up is the 4 on 3 situation. Run the same system again – you will find this is quite demanding and soon improves the fitness of the team.

FAST BREAKS WITH MORE PLAYERS

The next series of drills puts a little pressure on the body, has competitive spirit and looks for a good fast-break system. You can have four players as an offensive side and two players at one end of the court in defence and three players at the other end of the court. Alternatively, you can just implement a 4 on 2 situation, with two defensive players at one end and two at the other. You can also work with five offensive players and three defensive players at one end and three at the other; or five offensive players and four defensive players at one end and three at the other. Whatever set-up you adopt, try to have fewer defensive players, and so an easier fast-break situation, at one end than the other (*see fig 133*).

Drill 13
The offensive team has two minutes to play and they are always on attack. Every basket scored is worth two points or three points if it is a three-point shot. If offensive players are fouled they come out of bounds and the clock is stopped. Every time the defence grabs the rebound, they must put the ball on the floor and the offence then have to pick it up and run to the other end immediately and try to score there. After two minutes the players reorganize themselves and change positions so defence becomes offence

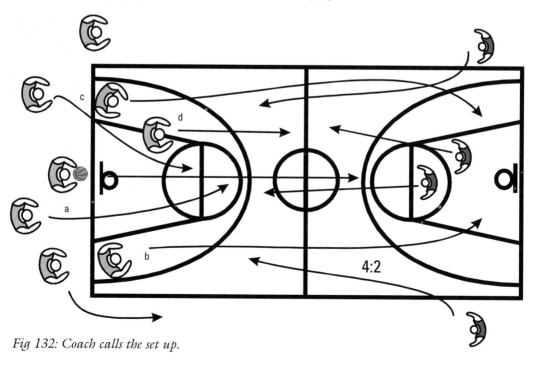

Fig 132: Coach calls the set up.

2 Minutes

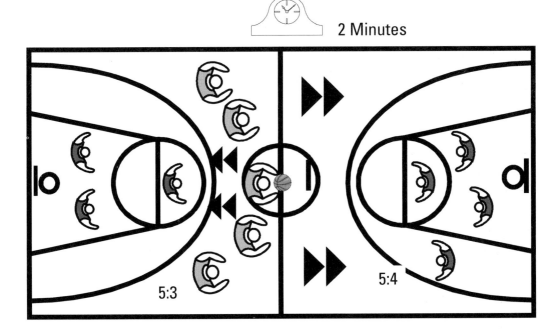

5:3

5:4

Fig 133: A two-minute read-run-execute drill.

and the offensive team divides to the defensive spots. During the two minutes of play every player plays and has to face very different kinds of situations. To make things harder, the defensive team can come up to half court so that they try to slow down the break from half court as well as disturbing the offence when they bring the ball up.

This is a full-court workout, which requires the players to be good at spotting each other and passing and, of course, make full use of the number advantage.

So why is the fast break so important in basketball? It is because more often than not a team does not have that many tall players, so uses speed to compensate for the height advantage of the opposition. Such teams are relying on a very aggressive defence, and good box-out and rebounding skills to give them the opportunity to score as quickly as possible from the fast break or the secondary break. The secondary break is when the team's trailer (the last two players down court on a fast break) follow the break itself and become a scoring option for the offence.

So for the team that opts for speed as a primary weapon, it is run, run, run all the time. Needless to say, the players have to be in top physical condition.

CHAPTER 7

Fitness and Footwork

Now that you have been introduced to all the game fundamentals, it is time to look at the other big issue you need to consider if you intend to play at all seriously – the issue of fitness and footwork.

Fitness is related to footwork and, of course, to aerobic endurance too. You have to be able to keep your knees bent for a long time and be explosive as required while you are running up and down the court. You must have court awareness and make the right decisions, and if you last longer physically and are very fit it is easier to maintain concentration and you have a better chance of winning the game. Fitness has an impact on the execution of all skills and fundamentals as well as on your psyche and your decision making, so do not ignore it. As always, the trick is to find the most effective way to improve fitness.

For an ambitious player who works a lot on his own, a cheap and highly effective investment is a skipping rope. This tool is used by many coaches, and in the series of drills and exercises below you will soon learn how demanding this 'children's toy' actually is.

The drills start off simple and then become more difficult. The load can be increased by the lengthening the distances you have to cover. If you follow through this series you will notice a huge improvement in your muscle control and general co-ordination as well as well as in your general fitness. A skipping rope session should last between 25 and 45 minutes.

SKIPPING ROPE DRILLS

Skipping rope drills are ideal for fitness work, improving co-ordination and focusing special attention on footwork, which is very important in basketball, both in defence and offence.

Even at senior level, however, these drills prove very difficult for some players. Not for everybody but for some. Traditionally, people play with the skipping rope while standing in one place, and these drills start with skipping on the spot for a minute and a half, a minute or 30 seconds. But basketball is footwork-orientated so we have to develop a different kind of skipping rope drill moving about the court, using the lines as guides. Of course the drills can be adapted to suit the required level. As players get more and more used to the skipping rope they improve dramatically, so the drills can be made more difficult. Your coach will spot when the drills are becoming easy for you and only then will he increase the difficulty.

It is also important that you use a good-quality skipping rope so that you do not have to struggle to hold it properly. It is also vital that the rope is the right length – not too short for tall players and not too long for younger or smaller players.

Take a look at the basketball court itself. There are a number of options for doing the skipping rope drills using the lines on the court:

1. You can do the drill on the baseline while walking at the sideline or at the baseline

walking on the sideline. This is the most basic pattern, recommended for very young players or beginners.

2. You can start alternating: do the drill on the sideline, walk on the baseline, do the drill on the sideline again and walk on the baseline back to the spot where you started.

3. With exceptionally good teams the drills can be done diagonally across the court from one corner to the other, the players then walking across the baseline and doing the drill diagonally back again.

4. All the players can line up together at the baseline and do the drill across the court, parallel with the sideline. When they arrive at the baseline they turn around, rest for a few seconds then repeat the drill back across the court.

The drill can be easily extended. For example, you can start on the baseline, walk on the sideline and then the baseline again, so you do the same drill at the two baselines, then at the two sidelines – or twice across the court or back and forth.

If the team does not have much time to spend on working with the skipping rope, then you can vary the drill. When one sideline is done they walk on the baseline to the other side of the court and continue to work on the other sideline. The first player demonstrates, the others will follow. When all the players have done one length from baseline to baseline, the coach can change the drill. Ideally you should try to fit in at least two lengths, though the drill can of course be extended to four or six lengths, or whatever the coach feels appropriate (*see fig 134*).

The Basic Skipping Drills

1. Run forwards, and turn the rope forwards (*see fig 135*).
2. Turn the rope backwards as you run forwards.

3. Bring your feet together and, as you turn the rope forwards, jump forwards (*see fig 136*).
4. Turn the rope backwards and jump forwards with your feet together.
5. Run backwards as you turn the rope forwards.
6. Run backwards as you turn the rope backwards.
7. Jump backwards with your feet together as you turn the rope forwards.
8. Jump backwards with your feet together as you turn the rope backwards (*see fig 137*).

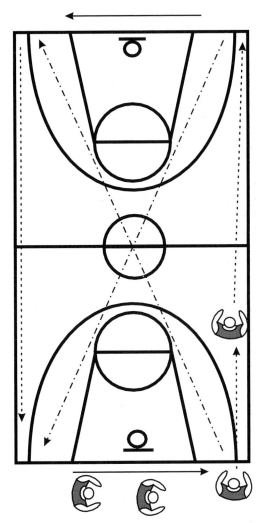

Fig 134: Moving patterns on the court.

Fig 135: Rope forwards, run forwards.

Fig 136: Rope forwards, jump forwards.

9. Jump onto your right foot as you turn the rope forwards. Then jump forwards.
10. Jump onto your left foot as you turn the rope forwards. Then jump forwards.
11. Jump forwards onto your right foot as you turn the rope backwards.
12. Jump forwards onto your left foot as you turn the rope backwards.
13. Jump backwards onto your right foot as you turn the rope forwards.
14. Jump backwards onto your left foot as you turn the rope forwards.

15. Jump backwards onto your right foot as you turn the rope backwards.
16. Jump backwards onto your left foot as you turn the rope backwards.

Those are the basic skipping moves. Now try some variations.

17. Turn the rope forwards and jump forwards twice on the left foot then twice on the right foot, followed again by the left foot. Do not stop between jumps (*see figs 138–139*).
18. Do the same thing but this time turn the rope backwards.
19. This time turn the rope forwards as you go backwards, and do two jumps on the left foot, then two on the right foot, then another two on the left foot.
20. Do the same thing but this time turn the rope backwards.
21. Face into the court and move sideways as you turn the rope forwards (*see fig 140*).
22. Do the same drill, this time turning the rope backwards.

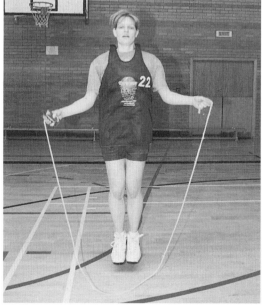

Fig 137: Rope backwards, jump backwards.

Fig 138: Rope forwards, jump forwards twice on the left foot...

23. Now face away from the court and move sideways as you turn the rope forwards.
24. Do the same drill, this time turning the rope backwards.

Building on the Basic Drills

Now it is time to play with the pace a little bit, as in a real basketball game. The following adaptations can be applied to all 24 basic drills.

25. Start at the baseline and work up the sideline forwards or backwards towards the half court; stop at the half court for 5 or 6 seconds, while keeping the rope movement going, then continue on to the baseline.
26. You can increase the number of stops, for example stopping first at the baseline, then at the foul line, then half court, then other foul line, before coming back the other way.
27. Now move to the first foul line, back to the baseline, to half court, from half court back to the foul line, from the foul

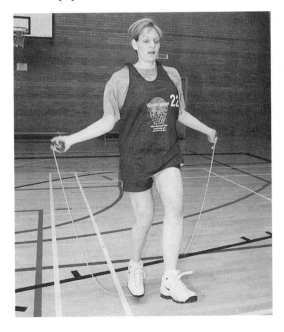

Fig 139: ...then twice on the right foot.

Fig 140: Rope forwards, move sideways.

line to the other foul line, then back to half court, from half court to the baseline, from the baseline back to the foul line and finish back at the baseline. This would be the most difficult, toughest, tiring sets of drills.

If you make a mistake try to get going again as quickly as possible. If many players are skipping together in a queue, a player who makes a mistake must step out towards the middle of the court so that the others on the

---

Skipping – Child's Play?

Coaches must be prepared for some resistance when they first introduce the concept of skipping rope drills. At the start they may find that the players are embarrassed, that they complain the drills are childish, that they are cannot do the drills properly and make many mistakes, even at senior level. But with encouragement the players improve rapidly and also gain in confidence when they see they can do the drills rather than just abandoning them and admitting defeat. Never admit failure and give up a teaching point.

---

sideline can carry on undisturbed. When the player is ready to restart the drill, he simply skips to the baseline and rejoins the others.

A good way to finish a block of skipping ropes drills is with a full speed run at top speed across the court. This is like a diagonal sprint with a skipping rope.

Alternatively, two or three pairs of players stand along the court at the middle and each pair has a skipping rope which they can turn in whatever direction they choose. All the other players line up at the baseline and then have to run through all skipping ropes adapting their speed so that they can weave between the spinning ropes easily (*see fig 141*).

Like all the other drills in the book these skipping ropes drills are flexible. If you were to do each of the drills described here just once you would still take up more floor time than you set aside for them. Be selective, and do not start with the most difficult one. Remember you always have the option of simply skipping on the spot in the traditional way, or doing runs for a specified time, for example three sets of 2 minutes or a 5-minute period, occasionally speeding up.

Fig 141: Adapt your speed.

As with everything else, the skipping rope drills can be adapted to create competition between individuals or between teams. This is especially effective with younger children because at beginner level fun is very important – and physical work can be fun to some extent. It depends how skilful the coach is who is conducting the session. Using the skipping rope is an intense activity; the lazy ones cannot escape the exercise because the rope forces them to work. The only option open to shirkers is to cheat a little bit on the distance, changing directions a bit too early. Those missed metres add up, and you could find at the end of the session that the lazy ones have done considerably less than the others, which could cost the team in the next game. The bottom line is that footwork is of the utmost importance in basketball and the skipping rope helps to improve footwork from a very early age.

AN AEROBIC ENDURANCE

At any point in the game the play could suddenly accelerate to the level where you have to run up and down several times as fast breaks follow each other, which is very demanding physically.

The Suicide Drill

The best-known drill to every player is the 'suicide', which involves running from the baseline to the foul line, then down to the baseline, then to the half court, back to the baseline again, to the other foul line, back to the baseline, to the other baseline and back. You should be able to do this in 30 seconds, but of course it depends on your age and fitness. To make it even more demanding, try doing two sets in a row in 60 seconds (see fig 142).

Sprint Runs

Another good training tool is sprint runs.

1. Run back and forth from baseline to baseline at full speed.
2. Have a 15-second break.
3. Do two more runs back and forth, then have another 15-second break.
4. Repeat steps 1 to 3 twice more.
5. Go back and forth twice more before a final 15-second break and a final sprint back and forth.

This is a very demanding drill. You can adjust the rest time to match basketball rules.

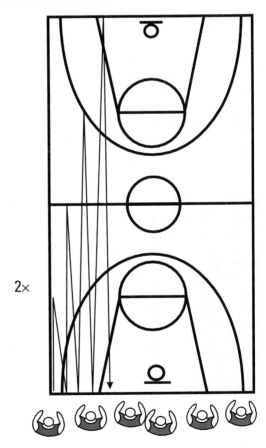

Fig 142: Suicide runs.

1. Sprint back and forth then rest for 5 seconds.
2. Now do the same but rest for 10 seconds.
3. Now do the same but rest for 15 seconds.
4. Now do the same but rest for 20 seconds.
5. After the next run rest for 24 seconds as in an offensive break.
6. Now work back down again, resting for 20 seconds after the sprint, then 15, then 10 and finally 6 seconds. This constitutes a full round.

Defensive drills are covered in Chapter 9, but one of them, the 'killing lanes' is an important part of fitness work, so can easily be incorporated into a fitness session.

AEROBIC ENDURANCE

Aerobic fitness is also very important for boosting stamina, and players will often ask questions such as 'Should I run 10–15km to increase my fitness and endurance?' Every kind of workout you do will help improve fitness, but you should always try to select the training method that will most help your basketball game. Basic aerobic endurance is important but you cannot acquire it overnight. Do not start with runs of 10 or 15km; usually the most you should do is about 3,200m or a 12-minute run. This should be gradually decreased to a series of 800/400m middle-distance runs. The most important part of the fitness programme is the 3 x 400m run, with a one-minute break after 400m. You should have a target time to complete the set; you do not have to run at maximum speed but you must try to finish within that time limit. This can be followed by speed drills, where you start with a 100m sprint, then work down to 60/30/15m sprints. All in all, a carefully designed track and field programme is extremely helpful.

WEIGHTLIFTING

All players want to improve their vertical leaps, and upper body strength helps you to win close body contacts and take positions. Therefore weightlifting is an integral part of preparation for a basketball player but this would take a whole other book to cover in proper detail; your best option is to consult specialist fitness guides.

CHAPTER 8

Defence

Defence is not the players' most popular part of the game, but defence wins the game while offence sells the ticket. In a good team defensive effort is valued very highly and defensive specialists are 'high trade value' for coaches.

Defence is not something you can practise on your own. Defensive drills need a coach, a motivator who pushes you.

THE PRINCIPLES OF MARKING

There are three basic rules you must keep in mind when playing in defence:

- Bend your knees to keep your weight low.
- Always maintain contact with the ground, so you can change directions quickly and follow your player.
- Use your hands to disturb, deflect or prevent a shot or pass (*see fig 143*).

When you mark a player it affects where you position yourself. You have to 'scout' your opponent to plan your strategy. Questions you should be asking about your opponent include:

- What are his favourite spots to shoot from on the court?
- Is he a good penetrator?
- Which side does he likes to go on more?
- How does he play without the ball?
- How does he read defence?
- Is he faster than you?
- Is he stronger than you?
- How is his rebounding and transition?
- What are his team mates expecting from him?

Once you have assessed your opponent you can build up your defensive strategy. Your physical abilities compared to your opponent will tell you where to position yourself. Defensive positioning is crucial. In principle, your aim is to put yourself between the player you are marking and the basket. However, when your opponent does not have the ball it is a good idea to stay a little bit towards the ball side rather than between him and the basket. Ideally you should also be able to point at both the ball and the player you are marking; if you can see both of them your position is right unless you are told differently by your coach.

Fig 143: In defence, your weight should go low.

97

When a player is faster and more athletic than you, correct positioning is even more important. In this case you have to leave a little bit more room between you and your opponent so that you can follow his moves, even at the risk that he might be able to take an outside shot.

If your player has the basketball, it is vital that you do not react to the fake: if you jump up as a result of an offensive fake you have no chance to change direction or to follow your player. To help you with this, always look at your opponent's belly rather than the basketball. Do not look after a pass made by the player whom you do marking: he may use your momentary distraction to shake you off and score.

Your priority at the end of your team offence is to locate your opponent as quickly as you can, and establish presence and body contact within the limits of the rules. You must be aggressive and force him to places on the court that he least likes and moves that he is not confident in doing. You must frustrate him with your presence (*see fig 145*).

Your should focus on your player, but you must still be able to see what is happening in other parts of the court because you may have to help your team mates.

ABOVE LEFT: John Amaechi is guarded very closely.

OPPOSITE: Delme Herimenn gets defensive help.

Fig 145: Focus on the player whom you are guarding.

Defensive Drills

The following defensive drills practise all these points, and also serve as footwork conditioning drills. The intensity of defensive play requires endurance – your feet must be ready for hard work.

Drill 1 – The Killing Lanes

Each line lasts for 24 seconds – the offence time.

Line 1. Digging.
Line 2. Digging and turning 45 degrees for the coach's signal.
Line 3: Digging and turning 45 degrees and bouncing back for the coach's signal.
Line 4: Digging and 'charging': lie down on the floor and stand up quickly for the coach's signal.
Line 5: Digging and jumping for shot block for coach signal.
Line 6: Digging and combining all previous tasks for coach signal.
Line 7: Digging (*see fig 147*).

Drill 2 – the Zigzag Drill

The players practice footwork on an imaginary Z path attached to each other on the court parallel to the sideline. When you turn your foot should never lose contact with the floor, otherwise you risk the offence changing direction while you are airborne and beating you. This drill's main task is to practise this.

- You must not cross his feet while shuffling.
- Drop your trailing foot by 45 degrees and reverse the position of your hands when changing direction.
- Always maintain contact with the floor when changing direction.
- Stay low all the way.

This is the basic defensive footwork drill (*see fig 148*).

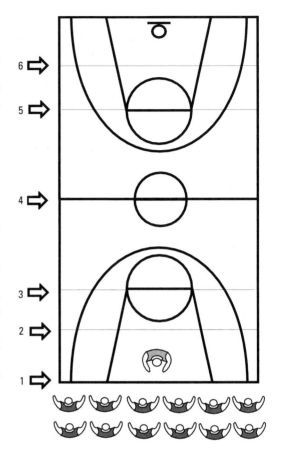

Fig 147: The killing lanes.

Drill 3 – Follow-the-Move Drills

You also have to mark players even when they do not have the ball. This means firmly establishing your presence and following them like a shadow. Offence players must always feel that they are closely guarded. This is the focus of the next drill.

Many courts have additional lines which can be useful for practices. There are various ways this drill can be done but the basic rules always apply. As the defensive player, you are not allowed to step into the 'corridor' set by the coach, while the offensive player, whose movements you are following, cannot step out of the 'corridor'. The corridor must be a narrow one (*see fig 149*).

You must stay very close to the offensive player; body contact is allowed, but holding back by hand is not. You have a basketball but your opponent does not. Keep the ball on his body while moving. You may push the offensive player when the ball is in contact but cannot hit him.

The offence must go through the other half within 8 seconds and work on the defence for about another 12 seconds (*see fig 150*).

Guarding Quick Players

When you have to guard an exceptionally quick player who is always in the fast break, you must locate him as soon as your team

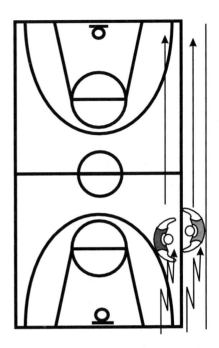

Fig 149: Follow your partner.

Fig 148: The zig-zag drill.

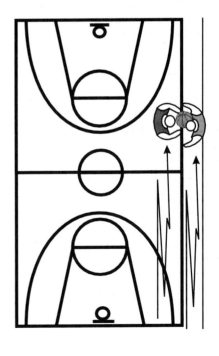

Fig 150: Follow and maintain contact.

The defence is working hard on Ronnie Baker.

BELOW LEFT:
Fig 152: Focus on the ball.

finishes the offence, and, while retreating, try to position yourself close to him. This is called 'fanning out'. The defensive transition moment, which is the move from offence back to defence, is crucial and can force the offence to play 5 on 5 rather than achieve an easy basket as described in Chapter 7. The next drill works on this.

Drill 4 – Run-Back Drill
Roll the ball on the floor for yourself, run after it, overtake it and retreat, 'playing' defence on the rolling ball (*see figs 152–154*). Options:

- Another player rolls the ball so you cannot control the transition speed
- You execute a lay-up, and a partner under the basket rolls the ball immediately
- After you have overtaken the ball, force it towards the sideline with little 'slaps' (*see figs 155–157*).

Fig 153: Cover one side more...

Fig 155: Touch the ball...

Fig 154: ...and retreat.

Fig 156: ...and force it towards the sidelines.

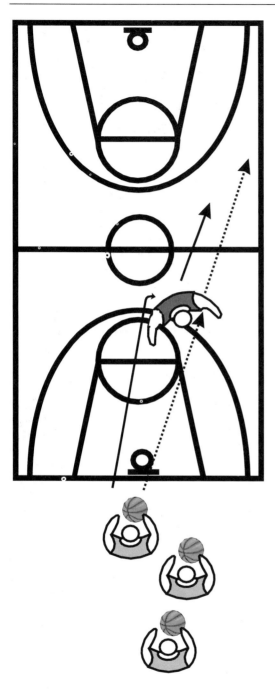

Fig 157: Defensive transition against a rolling basketball.

Mostly when you play tough, tight defence against a player who is crucial for the offensive team he will try to get rid of you at all costs. You may face a series of screens set by that player, so you have to have options in defence just like in offence; when you receive screens you may slide, go through the screen and follow your player, or ask for a switch, which means a team mate will take your player while you will take your team mate's player. This aspect of defence is called 'defensive communication' and is an important part of teamwork.

Drill 5
You and a partner each roll your own basketball on the floor, then run after it to overtake it and retreat to the baseline 'playing' defence

Fig 158: Talk to each other.

Fig 159: Locate and mark your ball.

on the rolling ball. If you cross each other's paths, defensive communication can take place. You can:

- Switch – touch each other and then play defence on the other basketball
- Slide – one of you gives room for the other to follow his basketball.

The same options apply as in Drill A (*see figs 158–160*).

CO-ORDINATING THE DEFENCE

The offence, which is favoured by the rules of the game, may beat you; they may pass you even without the screen being successful or as a result of a quarter of a second's lack of concentration on your part. You must know when to call for help – help means that one of your team mates, usually the closest, one will leave his man and try to stop your offensive player. But do not forget you have to recover as quickly as possible so that the team regains its defensive balance. A big part in

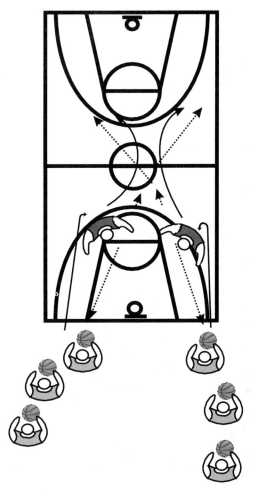

Fig 160: Two men defensive transition and communication.

defence is your attitude. Do you really want to stop somebody? If you do, you will contribute a great deal to the team's overall success. Every time that you do a defensive drill, think about how you will do it, how you will apply this particular drill or training point during an actual game.

You cannot think only about yourself in basketball. This is a team sport and the defence is part of the team effort. In man-to-man defence you may need help when you get into trouble and the situation is difficult. For example, you have the ball, which you must

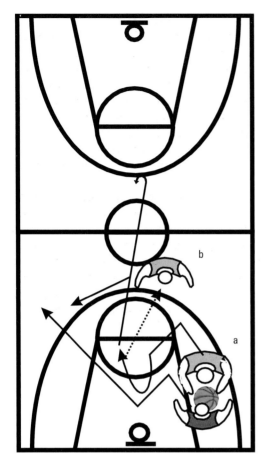

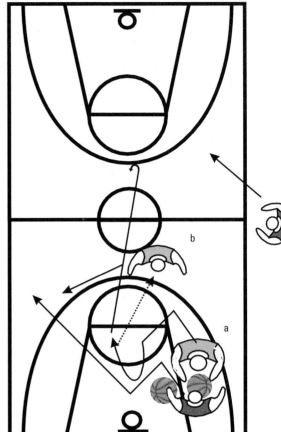

Fig 161: You need help in defence.

Fig 162: Defence needs decisions, too!

keep in contact with the offensive player. If things start getting difficult you may pass the ball to a team mate, who then takes over the job of keeping the ball in contact with the offensive player. Meanwhile, you cut back and take up a strategic position because the same situation might reoccur *(see fig 161)*.

Drill

Now both offence and defence have a basketball. Your defence task is the same as in the previous drills, but this time an additional offensive player stands at half court. He joins the offence when the ball

carrier crosses the half court lane – not earlier – and he may score, but only one pass is allowed *(see fig 162)*.

ZONE DEFENCE

The basketball court can be divided into zones which are made up of territories, and every player is responsible for certain territories. Different zones can be used depending on which area you want to secure. The principle of the zone is that the defence aims to outnumber the offence in certain areas while giving up other areas where they have found their opponents to be weaker. The most traditional is the 2/3 zone, where the defence protect the rebound and the restricted area known as the paint, while the offence are allowed to outnumber the defensive players on the perimeter. This does not mean that you do not defend those players and let them shoot freely, it just means that when the offence turns to the weakest part of the zone the defenders might have to work a little bit harder and run more than they would do in a simple man-to-man defence. In the 2/3 zone, the defence establishes its presence under the basket and your priority is to cover close range shots and secure the rebound.

Zone defence requires communication between defenders, good footwork and a lot of practice. Unfortunately, many teams of younger players are using the zone defence because they are not good at shooting from outside, so have the idea that staying on their knees in the zone rather than doing any hard footwork is a proper defensive concept.

CHAPTER 9

The Positions: Guards, Forwards and Pivots

Guards and forwards are very important in the back court (perimeter) area of the court. Without an effective back court your team cannot operate well throughout the whole 40 minutes of the game. Without an effective back court you give the defence a chance to pack underneath the basket, guarding your tall players, regardless of the rest of the team.

The pivot – or the centre, or big man – is distinguished by his size and power and his rebounding ability. As a team, you can do much better with a good big man.

In the modern game the point very often comes under heavy defensive pressure, so it is important that the off guard (no. 2) has the ability and the skills to take over the point guard's duty occasionally. This means being able to offload the pressure on the point, and still run the team continuously without serious problems. Needless to say, if both guards pose a consistent outside threat at both positions, this makes the team very effective against all kind of defences, and also makes it much easier for the big man to operate under the basket by giving him more room.

Forwards should be good shooters, precise and reliable in the execution of lay-ups, quick in the fast break, and good at passing to the posts and driving to the basket.

TRAINING THE BACK COURT PLAYERS

All these back court players participate in the team practices so they do the team drills, the fast break drills, the tactical drills, the defensive drills, and, of course, they participate in the fitness programme – they are virtually the backbone of the team. This does not mean that they do not benefit from individual sessions and drills created for them, which improve their ability on the particular court where they are playing. Most coaches envy European back court players, whose excellent passing and outside shooting are ideal for building a team offence. To achieve these standards, you cannot rely on simple shooting drills alone in the individual sessions, but must practise passing, dribbling, and then shooting. In these practice sessions it is always important that the players compete. If there are three to five players present, they compete against each other; if there is only one, he is set a target – either a certain score to achieve or a time limit – and he then competes against himself. It is helpful if to record these results so the player can follow his progress throughout the season or any period of time.

The next question is how often should you have individual sessions. Essentially, the more you practise the better you get. Amateur players can seldom increase the number of practices without cost, but a one-off session or two will not make you a significantly better player. The sessions must be regular. Then again, the coach is probably unable to contribute the extra time because he is not paid and has another job, but if he teaches the drills to the players then they can do it by themselves or with one or two partners and record the score so that then the coach can follow their progress. Ultimately, in amateur basketball it is impossible to make significant progress without the players' co-operation.

Another frequently asked question is 'Should we separate the players and do different drills during team practice?' If you have enough practice sessions in the week then this is probably a good idea; and if you have an assistant coach, you can arrange that he takes the periods for the guards and forwards and sets work for them at one basket.

For individual practice it is essential that everybody has at least one basketball, and for certain drills you will need more than one.

In pure shooting drills we emphasize the quick shot release that is crucial in the back court. There are specific shooting drills for forwards, for guards and for pivots, where the importance is not just how many baskets are scored but how quickly the player reaches that target or within what time limit he has to score more and more baskets. This approach encourages speed in shooting. When you shoot, you will not always shoot from the same spot. In a modern game you rarely shoot from the same spot five or six times in a row. In fact, if you do, you will probably find your team mates getting very impatient. Therefore constant movement between shots is an important feature of every drill.

Other drills work on other aspects of the game, such as passing, dribbling, distributing the ball, vision on a half court, and so on; but all drills should end with one or two shots because, regardless of where you are, in offence you must be a threat to the basket. When the defence allows enough space to shoot or penetrate you must do it. There is nothing worse than a player who thinks his role is only defensive. All players have to know their role and their part in building up the offence – for example, providing proper screens, passing down to the post, moving to empty spots, getting rid of the defence and

England's point guard, Ronnie Baker.

above all, keeping your defensive player busy. If you do not play without the ball it means your man can drop to half side and strengthen the opponents' defensive efforts, which is not at all desirable.

DRILLS FOR POINT GUARDS

Passing Drills

Drill 1
Look at Fig 164 now. A is the guard, who will do a 24-second passing series. B has a basketball on his left side and C has a basketball on his right side.

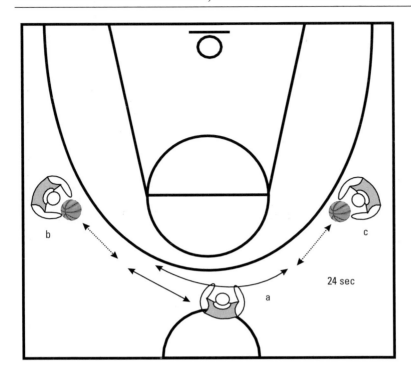

Fig 164: Point guard passing drill.

1. A runs towards B, stops, receives the ball and passes it back
2. A now moves to the other side, where he receives the ball from C, passes it back to him as quickly as he can, then turns immediately to B.

• It is vital that B and C do not hold the ball too long waiting for A to move towards them. They have to give him a real hard time in passing, distributing the ball back and forth within 24 seconds.

Drill 2

This drill is similar and also lasts 24 seconds. A stands at the point guard position without a basketball; B and C have a ball each.

1. A runs towards B, receives a pass from him and dribbles the ball to the other side.
2. He changes the basketball, passing his ball to C while quickly receiving C's pass.
3. He now drives the ball to B's side and does the same there. The players do not say in advance what pass they will use, but they have to do all the passes without any mistakes and without the balls hitting each other. If this happens the players have to start the drill again.

4. In Fig 165 you can see that after the 24 seconds expires, player A takes shots (on a signal from the coach) – one shot from the right side and one from the left. How he finishes is up to him. He may take a jump shot on the right side after dribbling, then receives the ball, dribbles back and shoots from the other side. This way he does not take two shots from the same spot and takes them from dribbling towards the wing side.

Drill 3

Players A, B and C each have a basketball. The drill lasts for 24 seconds.

1. A dribbles very briefly – fewer than two bounces is ideal – before passing the ball to B while receiving B's ball in exchange.

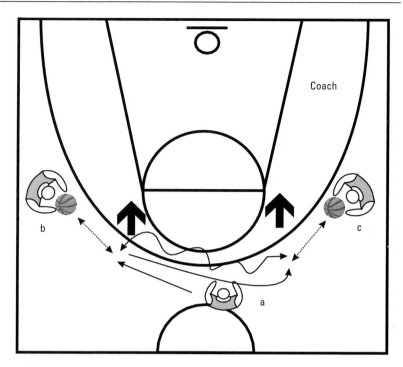

Fig 165: Back court pass-dribble-shoot drill.

2. A then turns to C and exchanges basketballs with him. The balls should not collide, either in the air or on the floor. You can set a target for the point guard to see how many balls he can distribute in the time.
3. After 24 seconds of heavy point guard duty A takes three shots; one with the ball he has just received, one from the other side, and then a final one with a ball he receives on the top in the point guard position, dribbles towards the middle and uses for a middle shot or a simple three-point spot-up shot (*see fig 166*).

Penetration Drills

Drill 4
A, B and C are at the half court, each with a ball.

1. A starts dribbling towards the point guard position.
2. He does two crossovers or a reverse and penetrates to score from the middle, releasing the basketball after scoring, then immediately running out of the three-point lane on the left wing side to receive a pass from B.
3. A now penetrates and scores from that side, leaving the basketball after the shot.
4. B runs under the basket and takes the first ball that A left after the lay-up.
5. A is now out at the other side and receives a pass from C, penetrates and scores. He picks up the ball and goes to the end of the line.
6. C picks up the second ball left by A after the penetration.
7. Now B carries out the same drill with a new player to replace A.

Drill 5
A stands in the middle, B and C on the left and right sides respectively. B has no basketball, but A and C have one each.

1. A passes his ball to the left side to B.
2. A moves, receives the ball from C, passes it back to him then cuts to the basket.

111

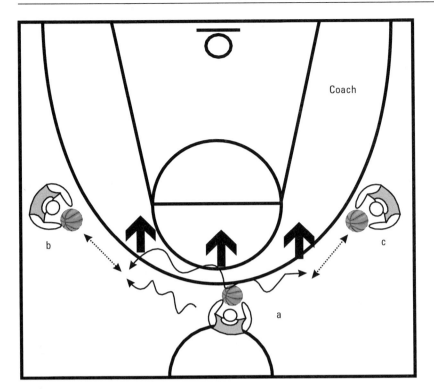

Fig 166: The 'three shots' point guard drill.

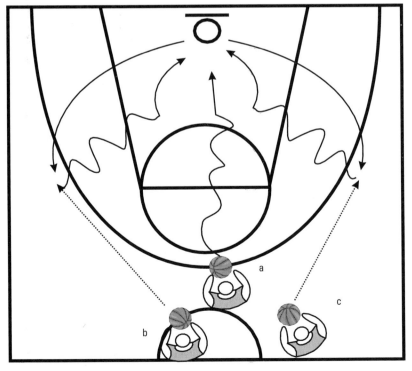

Fig 167: Penetration drill.

OPPOSITE: Fig 168: The wingman's work.

3. B passes the ball to A, who executes a lay-up. In the meantime, C dribbles his ball up to the point guard position.
4. Right after the lay-up, A moves out from the point to the wing, receives a ball from C and spots up for a mid-range or three-point shot.
5. Immediately afterwards he cuts through the paint to the baseline in the opposite corner, while B recovers the rebound from A's lay-up (at stage 3)
6. B passes the ball to the corner to A, who finishes the whole drill with a dribble penetration towards the baseline and scores.
7. When the whole drill has been completed the players rotate clockwise and get ready for the next player to do the drill (*see fig 168*).

DRILLS FOR FORWARDS

These special drills for forwards improve their skills on the wing side. Needless to say, every drill has to be done on both the left and right side of the court.

Drill 6
Players A, B and C stand in a queue, each with a basketball. One cone is placed down low towards the baseline, not far from the side of the paint.

A throws the ball up into the air, then runs down and comes outside the cone, catches the ball after one bounce and executes a jump shot. B and C do the same in turn.

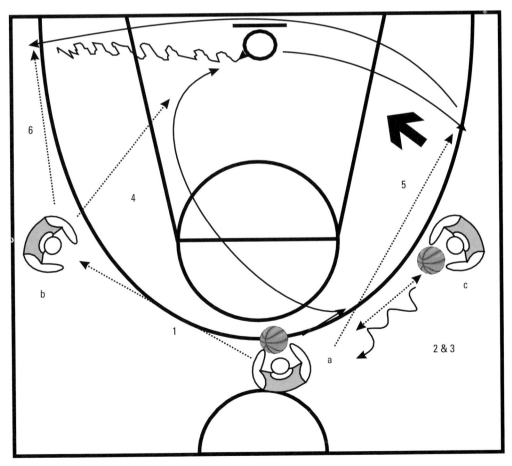

You can do the same drill finishing with a penetration rather than a jump shot. It is important to draw a line below which the drop cannot go so the wing man is forced to move at maximum speed. This is good practice for freeing yourself for a shot or penetration.

If you look at Fig 169 you can see that this drill would create that situation that very often happens on the wing man's side – after determined footwork you have got away from your defensive player but have not managed to lose him completely. Therefore you have gained just a small advantage and you must now use that advantage to surprise the defender with either a quick jump shot with a very fast shot release or a fake to put him up into the air and allow you to penetrate. Then the moment when the defender moves towards you at high speed – which happens very often in the game, for example after an in and out pass or after some good footwork on your part – gives him a little space to receive the ball comfortably and take the shot.

Drill 7
Repeat the drill above but this time add three other players (D, E and F) who wait in the opposite corner. When A drops the ball and goes down to go around the cone, D, E and F run at full speed across the paint to mark him. If A is quick enough, he can get a good jump shot in first. If he manages to gain just a small temporary advantage, then he can fake dribble penetration or fake secondary jump shot so that he can virtually play one on one. If he is not quick enough he comes under pressure and has to suffer to gain position under the basket *(see fig 170)*.

Drill 8
Now you can take the drill further. The players are set up as before, but there are now two additional two players who are always the same – X, who is always with the offence, and Y, who is defending X. When the ball is dropped and the opposite defender D comes towards A at full speed, A has the option to penetrate and pass to X. While A is looking

Fig 169 The wing decision time.

Fig 170: You must decide against defence.

for the lay-up or jump shot, it is possible that he can pass the ball to the post (X). Y, who is defending X, can, if he wants to, give help to D. This creates the typical situation that many wing men face, where they are challenged and have to pass the ball quickly to the post *(see fig 171)*.

Drill 9
This drill practises another typical situation – how to cut to the backdoor or go for a shot when you are overplayed. B is on offence with A, but C has the basketball at the start. C is marking B.

1. C passes the basketball to A at the point guard position and immediately takes an overplay (denial) position on B.
2. B tries to move out first for a shot but he is denied; he now has a great opportunity to go backdoor, or, if he is covered, he

still can come back for the shot or try the backdoor again. The first option is go backdoor.

For this drill you have to imagine a theoretical line that cuts the key in half from under the basket towards A; B cannot cross this line, or can cross it but cannot score from there. He has to get himself free in his particular corner of the basketball court *(see fig 172)*.

Drill 10
B plays in the same way as above, but if he cannot make a backdoor pass, he has two options: either to kick the ball out to A, who must execute a jump shot, or to penetrate and pass to his other wing man, D, who also then has to execute a jump shot. Immediately after recovering the rebound B goes back on offence and this play continues for one minute; the aim is to see which player scores the most baskets.

115

Fig 171: More decisions to make.

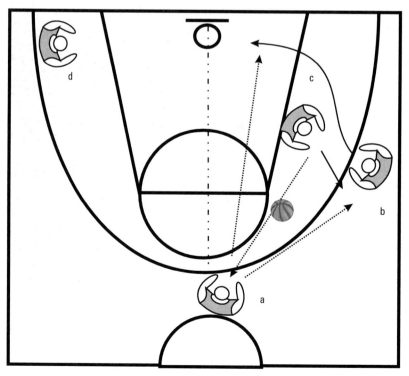

Fig 172: Go against overplay.

DRILLS FOR PIVOTS

Drill 11 – Drop, Step, Shoot

Stay back near to the basket. Step inside the paint, establishing a powerful inside position, bounce the ball close to your body once only, then jump up from both feet and score.

Use both left and right hands, then do the same from the opposite side (*see figs 173–174*).

Now do the same drill with somebody behind you pushing you with a soft mat or another basketball.

Players in the low post have to do these moves as well as drop steps upwards away from the basket, finishing with a baby hook shot (*see figs 175–176*).

Do the same drill finishing with a fade-away jumper. You can practise this shot from a dribble, but I would suggest a pass inside instead. That way you jump away from the defender and add some extra power to your shot execution to balance the distance.

ABOVE: *Fig 173: Drop step and ball protection.*

RIGHT: *Fig 174: Go up strong.*

Fig 175: Work against contact...

Fig 176: ...and cover the ball.

Andy Betts posts up.

Roger Huggins in post position.

Andy Betts goes strong under the basket.

Fig 183: The X drill executed inside the paint.

Drill 12 – The X-Drill

It is important to understand that when the pivot receives the ball inside the paint it does not necessarily mean that the ball has to go up.

1. The pivot has the basketball; he passes it to A and goes across the paint to high post.
2. He receives the ball from A and passes it to B, and goes to the low post on that side
3. He receives the ball from B and he passes it to A, then moves across the paint parallel with the baseline.
4. He receives the ball from A and executes a jump shot under the basket. This drill can be adapted in various ways depending on where we want the pivot to pass the ball. It is important that he changes his position after every pass out, moving across the paint or staying parallel with the baseline.

If he goes across the paint he usually goes from low to high or from high to low. If he moves across and parallel with the paint it usually means baseline moves. The main issue for an effective pivot is how, in limited space and tough circumstances, he can free himself and score (*see fig 183*).

Faking

The pivot starts in a low post position with one defender, while partners A and B are on the wing with one ball each. The pivot has to score with both basketballs; he can pass the ball back to A or B and can score whichever ball he wants first. The only restriction is that he must score with both basketballs, so if he is good at fakes and passes he will get rid of his marker very easily and have an easy basket.

CHAPTER 10

Man-to-Man Offence

We want to succeed, we want to score, but the defence is always there to stop us. Athleticism and physical abilities have taken over the game to the extent that it is now not plausible for one player to beat five. Therefore a team offensive strategy is necessary to combat man-to-man defence. This usually means the players having to set screens for each other and play for the moment when the defence makes a mistake, either by positioning themselves incorrectly, through poor communication or poor switching, or simply create a situation known as a 'mismatch'. This is where, for example, a shorter player has to guard a much taller player under the basket or a very slow, big player comes out and has to guard an exceptionally quick forward outside the perimeter.

SET OFFENCE

In the current basketball rules the offensive time is just 24 seconds. This means that if a team wants to play a set offence then they only have time for one set. There is now no time to set up a second time so you must have a simple end option in case nothing comes out of your set offence. You must play a simple give and go or pick and roll, and score from that.

The set offence is a series of screens created by the players for each other, and players should take the first available opportunity to score, penetrate or shoot from outside. The set offence is not designed to entertain the coach, it is designed to achieve a basket as quickly as possible. The team should not try to keep the set offence going until the last moment. Your focus should always be the basket and scoring. Scoring should be part of everybody's role in the team regardless of what position he plays, and when a player is free and the defence grants the opportunity he must use it.

Because of the time limit, the set offence should be simple, easy to execute and give players several options while building it up. If the defence is well organized and successful in guarding, then the set offence usually ends up with an option for one of the best players to score. The option has to be a double one in a set offence – one to score from inside, and one to put the ball in the hand of a good outside shooter or penetrator who can break the defence down.

Every player who plays set offence has to watch what happens all the time. You know what to do, but if one of your team mates suddenly changes the offence, you should not automatically consider it a human error. He judged the situation was such that he could try to score, and all the other players must read the game situation and move accordingly rather than continue the set offence.

The set offence is usually called by a signal from the point guard in the European game; it could be a number, body language or, if there is no noisy crowd, the point guard can simply call it. In the USA the coaches used to call most of the offences so the coach acquired the nickname 'play-caller'.

Whether you play offence or defence, you must be aggressive to accomplish and win.

MOTION OFFENCE

Motion offence is a virtually endless type of offence where the coach sets up certain rules that the players have to follow until they can find an ideal way to achieve an easy basket or spot up relatively undisturbed and take an outside shot. For example:

Rule 1: Pass the ball and cut to the basket. Other players move without the ball to keep good spacing fundamentals.

Rule 2: Pass the ball and screen away from the ball. Ensure correct setting of the screen. The player using the screen must read the defender and cut hard off the screen, moving shoulder to shoulder with the screener.

Rule 3: When reversing the ball, passing from the wing to the point, the player who has passed the ball must receive a back pick from the post player. After setting the back screen the post player must step high towards the ball.

PRACTISING SET OFFENCES

The coach's challenge is always how to make the teaching of tactical elements of the basketball game more intensive, particularly when there are many players in a practice session. The most important thing is to ensure that players do not simply switch off when they are not actually executing a drill, but look at the court and concentrate on what is going on. One system that tries to do this is the Magic 3 Pass drill, which starts with very simple exercises and goes on to become extremely complicated. The offence introduced here is particularly recommended for medium-level and junior teams.

The Magic 3 Pass Drill

The drill is designed to be done on half court but with two sides of the court working simultaneously, and on a higher level it could be a full court drill too. Although you are working on half the court, the distance that the players actually cover in this system is the same as one full court because with the Magic 3 pass – fully described below – they move out to the half court lane and then back towards the basket. So in one drill the players complete a full basketball court length, running, changing directions, looking and precisely executing the instructions given. Each drill is just a little different from the previous one. This is because the players start to go through the moves automatically after a while, so you have to add a change to keep them alert. Mental presence is as important as physical presence on the basketball court. Mental presence means that the player is able to understand his own movements, he can watch his team mates and while he is off the drill for a couple of seconds he is still capable of following his team mates' work and assessing or even helping them if it is needed.

The following drills build up a continuous offence from the Magic 3 Pass drill, but it can also be used to create a man-to-man offence, a set offence, a continuous offence or even a zone offence. It is even possible to incorporate defensive players. You might not be able to do everything in one practice session, but the system is effective and the learning time is

---

Monitoring Practice

The coach has to monitor the practice carefully. If an individual player makes the odd mistake, the coach can deal with it easily. However, if the same mistake keeps appearing, and is made by several players, it is advisable to stop the session in order quickly to underline and demonstrate the main points again, and then continue the practice.

---

significantly shorter than with more traditional ways. On the other hand, it is more tiring, requires a higher level of concentration and, despite the fact that there is no particular physical pressure, some players sweat more than during suicide runs. The drills help players to learn correct positioning and good timing.

Do not try to progress from the beginning right through to the complete offence in one session. It could be very tiring, it could even be boring and lose its appeal. It is up to the coach to judge how many drills he can use in one practice, how many he will repeat next time and how quickly he wants to progress. Of course, it is also true the players will not benefit much if you do a set of drills one day, then do not do the others for a month and then suddenly expect the players to understand the next step. Planning is vital at any level. Each drill has to be done on both sides: there is no point training a team that can only execute a set offence only towards the right or the left side. The team has to be able to cope if the defence shuts one side.

As with any set of drills that the players get to know well, once the players have learnt the easy Magic 3 drills and are practising the more complicated ones they start less care over the initial, familiar stages. The first three passes become slower and less precise, change of direction is not so sharp and the players are not as focused as they were at the start. The coach has to remind the players that precision is required from start to finish. Practice is not recreation.

The Opening Moves
Divide the team into two equal groups. Each group splits into pairs who gather, the partners facing each other, at both ends of the court under the basket. Each pair has one ball. In Fig 185 you can see players A, C and E are under the basket without basketballs just outside the end line where the paint meets with the end line. Opposite them are their partners, B, D and F, each with a ball.

1. A starts to run towards the half court. B passes the ball to him – first pass. 2. A receives it and without dribbling returns it to B, who also runs towards the half court – second pass.
3. B receives the pass and without stopping passes the ball back to A – third pass.
4. Both players are now between the half court line and the three-point lane of the basket. They stop, square up and look down to the basket they came from. Under the basket could be six, eight or even ten players, depending how many are present at the session.

This is the first step and this is how every single drill in the Magic 3 Pass system will start. How the drill finishes will vary every time.

Fig 185: The 'Magic Three Pass'.

Drill 1

This drill starts with the three passes as explained above.

1. This time, after A and B have done their three passes and look back to their basket, B does a backdoor cut to the basket, receives a pass – the fourth pass – from A and executes a lay-up.
2. A goes for the rebound, and changes places with B.
3. A, who now has the ball, joins the end of the queue of those players who have basketballs, while B joins the end of the queue of players without balls.

Drill 2

From now on the first three passes will not be marked on the diagrams, but the players must still do them. This drill adds an extra player.

1. After the three passes A and B square up. B does the backdoor cut, but A, instead of passing the ball to B, passes it to C, who is the next in the queue and now steps into the court to receive it.
2. C passes under the basket to B, who did the backdoor cut and now executes a lay-up.
3. A goes for the rebound and changes places with B, while C is ready to receive the first pass from his partner, D.
4. D and C will do their three passes, square up to the basket and execute the same drill (*see fig 186*).

Drill 3

1. B does the cut, then, as before, A passes the ball to C.
2. C fakes towards B.
3. B moves across the paint and sets a screen; A uses it, steps inside the paint, receives the ball from the corner and scores (*see fig 187*).

The players who are not on the drill have to look at what the players on court are doing. C has to step in at the right time,

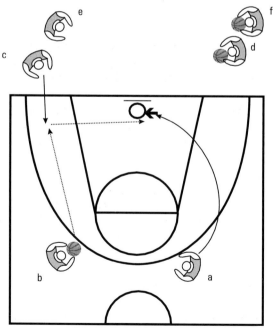

Fig 186: A backdoor cut.

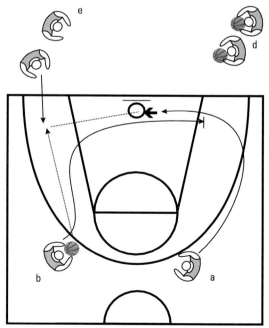

Fig 187: A screen after cut.

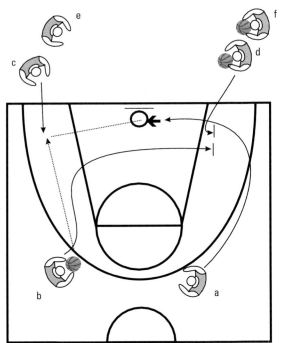

Fig 188: The double pick.

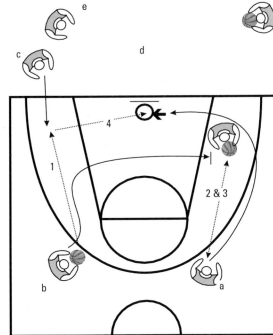

Fig 189: The 'timing' drill.

and when he makes the final pass to B he immediately has to look at his partner to start the next drill. His partner, D, must be alert as well, so he can pass the ball to C at the right time.

Drill 4
1. B does the cut, then, as before, A passes the ball to C.
2. C's partner, D, now steps in with a basketball in his hand, raises it high and takes a mid-post position.
3. A, instead of just doing a run and simple backdoor cut as he did on the previous drills, uses the passive block of D to move around and step into the paint
4. A receives a pass from C and scores.
5. A goes for the rebound, and A and B join the end of their respective queues, while D immediately turns towards C and starts the next drill (*see fig 188*).

Drill 5
The next drill introduces a timing pass because timing is a very important element of the offence. Steps 1 and 2 are as above.

3. When D is set at the mid-post position, B, instead of directly cutting, moves to the sideline outside the three-point lane and receives a pass from F.
4. B passes the ball back to F and then cuts through, steps into the paint, receives the ball from C and executes the lay-up. This could mean that C arrives a little bit later under the basket than in the previous drill (*see fig 189*).

Drill 6
Steps 1 and 2 are as in Drill 4.

3. B passes the ball to C as in the previous drills, then immediately cuts through the paint, showing himself ready to

receive to the ball and score if the opportunity arises; if not, he continues through the paint and sets a pick between the baseline and D.

4. A moves to the same spot where he previously did the timing pass but this time he will not receive a pass; when the double pick is set by D and B he uses the double pick step under the basket, receives a pass from C and scores.

Drill 7

The offence is almost ready now. This time we shall put a point guard (X) in the middle of the court.

1. A and B do their three passes.
2. A passes the ball to C and cuts through the paint to set up the double pick for B, who moved to the side.
3. Now X goes towards C, receives the ball and dribbles it to the middle; he also looks under the basket and might then pass it to D, who has just gone across using the double pick set by A and B.

4. While X is looking around ready to pass to anyone, C moves towards the paint and sets a pick to B again.
5. B steps out ready to shoot.

The Final Offence

Fig 190 shows the complete offence that we have built up.

1. It starts obviously from no. 1, the point guard, who passes the ball to the left.
2. No. 4, the low post, pops out to the corner.
3. No. 2 passes the ball to him and then immediately cuts through the paint.
4. No. 3 fakes and moves to the wing side, while number 5 is in the low post position.
5. Nos. 2 and 5 set up a double pick as practised in the drills.
6. No. 3 uses the double pick to step inside, looking to receive the ball from no. 4.
7. If it is not given to him, no. 4 passes off to the point guard, who flashes on his side and dribbles the ball to the middle.
8. Now it is up to the point guard where

Fig 190: The complete offence against man to man defence.

The ball must be kept in safe hands, ideally down low.

he will pass and how he will continue the offence. No. 4 goes back into post position and no. 3 can use him to move up to shooting position.

9. If the point guard decides to pass to the left to no. 3 the ball (look at the pass marked DA), no. 3 takes a shot.

10. The point guard could pass to no. 4 instead (pass DD), who posts up, but the same things happen on the other side as well, because from their other double pick no. 2 moves out to a shooting position. He may receive the ball from the point guard (look at pass DD) or no. 5 posts up and receives the ball (look at Fig 190, pass DC).

11. If none of them have the opportunity to do the job or take a free shot then the offence can start again. Any of the low posts pops out, receives the pass, cuts through for double pick, and the offence can carry on indefinitely.

Using the Magic 3 Pass drills will build up an offence very quickly, but it is up to the coach to adapt the drills to his own training system. Whatever he does with the drills, he can have an intensive, game-like practice, which is ideal.

CHAPTER 11
Zone Offence

The principle of this offence is to compress the zone into a small territory, since the zone defence's major task is to protect territories and players are responsible for their territories.

A zone offence requires a team that passes the ball around very well and can read the defensive position. The major goal is to break down the team defence as soon as possible. Zone offence in general consists of more passing than dribbling. The dribble is kept for the penetration, when the zone defence cannot follow the quick ball movement properly and the offence may utilize the gaps between the lines of the zone defence.

This could result in an easy lay-up or challenge, requiring help from other lanes of the defence. If this happens the spaces left open are free for use by the offence, who can step inside behind the defensive lanes. To achieve this, the offensive players have to do a lot of passing and move between the lanes.

In zone offence there is always a strong side and a weak side. On the strong side the offence normally outnumbers the defence, while on the weak side there are fewer offensive players. Players changing from these sides during the offence can also break the team defence.

ZONE OFFENCE IN ACTION

Look at Fig 191.

1. Offensive players nos. 2 and 3 step into the key while no. 1 (the point guard) has the basketball.

2. Nos. 4 and 5 also close in, in the low post positions. This is like compressing the zone into the paint.

3. The point guard decides which way he would like to go; if he goes to the right, the only movement that happens is that no. 4 starts to move parallel with the baseline aiming for the corner.

4. No. 5 sets a screen, trying to keep the defender inside so that when no. 4 reaches the corner and receives the ball from no. 1 he is relatively free to shoot if he wants to.

5. The moment that no. 1 picks up the ball everybody suddenly moves into shooting position. No. 4 arrives at the corner ready to shoot, while no. 3 moves out to the point guard position and no. 2 moves out at the other side on a wing guard position. No. 5 makes a small but decisive move, coming up from the low post to the mid-post position, facing no. 1 and ready to receive the ball.

6. This suddenly spreads the zone wide, and the point guard has to use his judgement to decide where to pass at this delicate stage. Experience shows that if the ball reaches no. 5, the zone moves in again and collapses. If no. 5 then either penetrates or passes the ball further out to the right spot, the offence have a good chance at a shot.

7. The options for no. 1 are to no. 4 to the corner, to pass to no. 5, to pass to no. 3, who puts it out to the point guard position, or to use a skip pass to the other

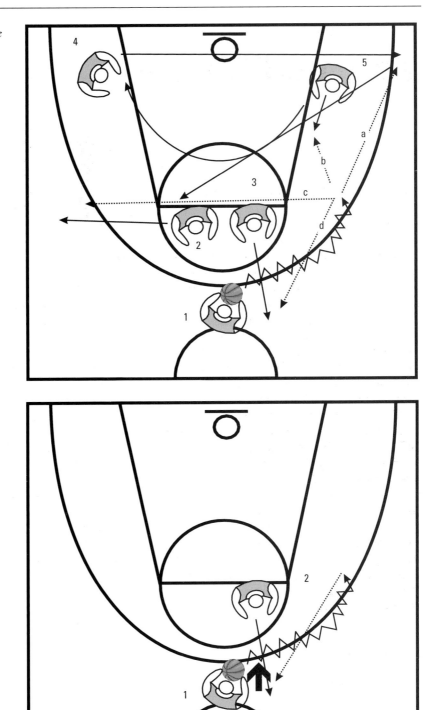

Fig 191: The complete offence against zone defence.

Fig 192: Dribble; Pop out.

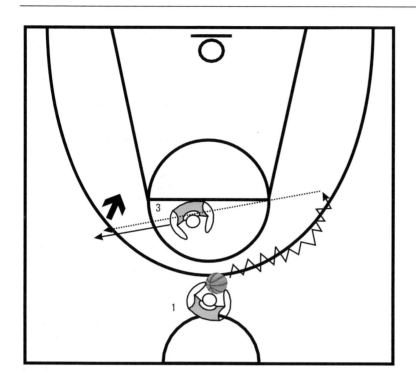

Fig 193: Dribble; Pop out; Skip pass.

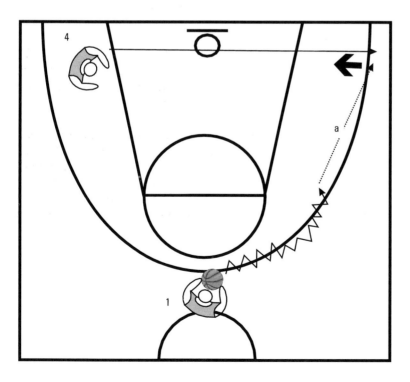

Fig 194: Pivot moves across.

side and pass the ball to no. 2. If no. 2 receives the ball, a direct pass o after swinging the ball around, then the pivot move is next. The principle is to move from high to low and from low to high, which in practice means no. 5 goes from mid post across the paint to the low post position on the side where no. 2 is, and no. 4 goes across the paint from the corner to the elbow, where he takes the high post position. As the ball moves around, the players consistently follow this pattern, rotating from high to low and from low to high. Within 10–14 seconds, if the ball is moving well, the offence will either have nice penetration opportunities or a good spot-up shot – which is the main aim of a successful zone offence.

BREAKDOWN DRILLS

Drill 1
Player no. 1 starts with the ball in the point guard position. His partner no. 2 is in the key. No. 1 dribbles the ball to the right side and when he picks it up his partner moves out, replaces him at the point guard position, receives the basketball, spots off and shoots (*see figs 192–193*).

Drill 2
This drill starts the same as above but no. 2, instead of moving up to the point guard position, now goes out to the other side to forward position, receives a skip pass and spots off and executes a jumper (*see fig 194*).

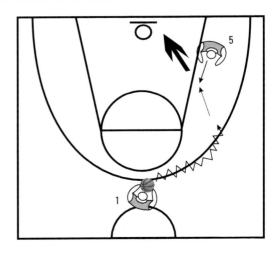

Fig 195: The mid post move.

Drill 3
The point guard starts with the basketball again, this time with player no. 4 at low post position. When the point guard starts to dribble the ball, no. 4 moves across, receives the basketball and executes a jump shot from the corner (*see fig 195*).

Drill 4
This time, when the point guard starts dribbling, no. 5 moves to mid post, pulls up, receives the ball and immediately turns in and scores from underneath.

After you have done these four breakdown drills, you can put together the zone offence. You can play it against a 2-3 zone (two players in front of three). It is important that the players read the slight differences between the zones and find out through practice who has more chance to score from the offences.

CHAPTER 12

The Foul Shot

Almost every team sport that has a penalty shot in the rules has a scope for high drama when all of a team's work and effort hang on a penalty shot. A missed penalty that could decide the team's fate can have a huge psychological impact on the player who missed it.

Many players go on the line at the crucial moment and execute a foul shot, which will have an impact on the final result. Pressure always mounts towards the end of each game.

If you know how to shoot a basketball then the foul shot is the kind of shot that you do not really need a coach for. You can practise it very simply if you put a flat surface under the basket; then every time you score from the foul line the ball bounces back to you. If you have a partner you can challenge your partner on the foul line and compete against each other.

The foul shot is not the same as a jump shot, but it is a good idea to practise it at the same speed and using the same technique as you do with your jump shot. The difference is that you remain on the floor. Do not do it slower or try to do something different; just do your standard jump shot that you would do standing on the floor undisturbed, with no defence in your face. The only thing that you have against you is the psychological pressure.

PRACTICE GAMES

There are several good team games that help players to deal with that psychological pressure. These fun but competitive games are a good way to end the practice session.

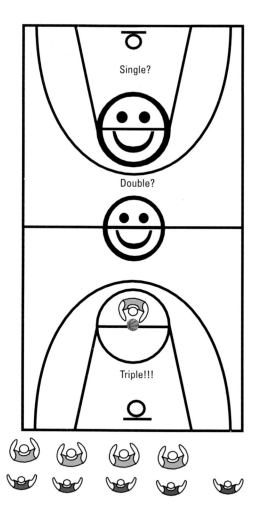

Fig 196: Do you want a bet?

The Sharp Game

All the players line up at the foul line and, one at a time, each take one foul shot. If the first one goes in, then the next player steps forward to the foul line and shoots. If this one goes in the coach calls 'the sharp', which means the third player must make the foul shot or he has to run one lap around the court. If he makes it, the number of laps climbs to two if the next player misses; if the next player makes it, the number of laps climbs to three and so on. The number of laps could go very high and tension rapidly builds up amongst the team because nobody likes to run while the others are laughing. If someone misses then of course he has to run as many laps as were called before the missed shot. If the first or second shot is missed there is no run and everything goes sharp when two consecutive shots go in.

All Run if you Miss

The whole team lines up on the baseline, and are called one after the other to the foul line to shoot. If the shot goes in there is no run, but if a player misses then everybody has to run one sprint back and forth. The game goes on until everybody has had a shot.

The Bet

In this version of the game, each player is allowed to bet on his own ability. He can bet single, double or triple. If he says 'triple' and makes the shot, then he and two other players whom he has chosen can sit out, but if he misses everybody, including him, has to run three sprints back and forth alongside the basketball court. If he makes a 'double' then he and one other player sit out, and for a 'single' just him. This game can become very interesting after two players have missed because then there is greater pressure and a conflict of interest. Many players want to get out, but on the other hand they do not want to have to run further sprints (*see fig 196*).

CHAPTER 13

A Final Word

If you have worked through all the drills in this book, you have already come a long way. So what comes next?

TEAM DEFENCE

Zone Defence

One thing you will need to practise is team defence. The simplest team defence is the zone defence, where you guard territories. This is unfortunately a very popular defence with younger teams because it gives them the kind of win they like, since shooting techniques are not very developed at an early age. In some European countries younger age groups are deliberately forbidden to play zone until they can easily break the zone defence. At international level, however, zone defence plays a big part, so you do have to spend time learning it.

Certainly a good zone defence is much more physically demanding than a man-to-man defence. A good team does not rest in defence; if the players need a breather they take it while they are in control of the ball. Despite the fact that the zone looks stationary, a good zone demands much more footwork and complex communication than simple man-to-man defence. The idea of the zone is that we give up certain parts of the court just to secure other areas.

The most common zone is the 2/3 zone. When you have to play against a team that has better perimeter players and far less effective inside players, you may instead choose to play a 3/2 zone. There is a 1/2/2, where the top man goes far out and almost always on the passing lane, which leads towards the point guard. Then there is the 1/3/1 zone, where the middle of the defence is a bit higher and the last man under the basket always moves to the side where the ball is.

Zone defence is also used often when the team is in dire trouble, because it always focuses on the ball and primarily follows the ball movements.

The Full Court Press

This can be either a man-to-man press or a zone press, and is used when a team is desperate to get the ball, or would like to run down an opponent because their fitness is superior or lacks depth.

In a full court press the object is to double team players at the sensitive points. When the opponents pick up the ball after dribbling, divert them towards the sideline, half court lane or baseline, where they could be trapped and from where it is difficult to pass the ball out. When they pass it out it is easier to steal and immediately go on a fast break at the other end. Of course, if you use a full court press then you also have to be well trained in the fast break.

COMPILING STATISTICS

It is now possible to record very detailed statistics during a game, so that you know, for example, how many points were scored

from how many attempts from different parts of the court, how many fouls there were and by which side, how many turnovers, steals and rebounds there were, and so on. Such statistics can be recorded both for the team and for individual players. At the end of the game, the points are added to the so-called IBM point system that rewards you for positive actions and deducts points for negative ones. This score is then divided by the time that you spent on court. The result is a figure that allows you to compare your performance with the other players'. For coaches, statistics make it possible to see how particular players are contributing to the team success.

If you want to progress you need drills, as the drills hone skills, and you need good skills to play well. It is simple to play in pick-up games, and even if you only play in these games you will improve. However, if you play in a well-organized and supervised team with a well-built system, your chances of succeeding are much greater. But ultimately it all comes down to practice: unless you practise regularly and work in drills you will never improve beyond recreational level. The choice is yours.

Only hard work will result in a breakthrough in basketball.

Glossary

Airball When a shot attempt is made and the ball does not reach its target, neither the basket nor the backboard.

Alive An attacking player who has the ball, but has not dribbled.

Assist A pass to an open team-mate that results in an immediate score. An excellent pass which find the team mate to score free, undefended.

Back Court That half of the court that contains a team's defensive basket.

Backdoor A term used to describe a cut by an attacking player towards the basket to the side of the defensive player away from the ball. It is mainly used when the attacking player is being overplayed or when the defence turns to look at the ball.

Back pick Screen that comes from behind the defensive player

Ball Control Game A type of attacking play that emphasizes maintaining possession of the ball until a good shot is possible.

Ball Side The side of the defensive formation close to the ball (see also help Side).

Bank Shot A shot in which the ball rebounds from the backboard to the basket.

Bat To use the flat of the hand to knock the ball away from a dribbler or ball handler.

Baseline drive A drive (see below) made close to the attacking end line of the court.

Blocking Personal contact that impedes the progress of an opponent who is not in possession of the ball (see rules).

Blocking out (boxing out/ cutting out) The positioning of a player in such a manner as to prevent an opposing player from moving to the basket to gain a rebound. The defensive player blocks (closes) the path of the offensive player to take a rebound.

Box and One A term used to describe a combination defence (q.v.) with four defenders playing a zone defence (q.v.) in a square formation (i.e. 2.2) with the fifth defender out chasing the ball or marking a particular opponent.

Break The rapid movement of a player to a space where they hope to receive a pass.

Bump Powerful body contact initiated by the defence when players without the basketball cut through the paint or screens. Brush off (Brush off screen) To cause one's opponent to run into a third player, thus losing them momentarily.

Buttonhook To move in one direction, turn sharply and double back.

Centre (post or pivot player) the name of one of the positions on the team, usually the tallest player, whose attacking role involves playing close to the opposition basket; usually they are the best rebounders. Their range is mostly close. If coaches talk about post they distinguish between high post and low post, which depends from the place they occupy under the basket.

Charging A personal foul, usually committed by an attacking player, caused by a player making bodily contact by running into an opponent.

Chaser A defender whose job is

to harass the attacking players. Usually the front player or players in a zone defence.

Circulation A player's movements about the court on attack.

Clear out An attacking manoeuvre versus a man-to-man defence, in which players vacate an area of court so as to isolate one attacking player and one defensive player. The attacking player may then attempt to score against this opponent, who has no defensive team-mates close enough to provide help.

Combination defence A team defence where some of the team members play to zone defence (see below) principles and others man-to-man defence.

Continuity play A team attacking system in which players move to one position and then another in a regular order, executing pre-planned play options in an endeavour to create a scoring opportunity. The attacking players' movements on court are so planned that they are used as the staring position for the next option.

Control Basketball (Possession Basketball) A style of play in which a team deliberately makes sure of every pass and only shoots when there is a very high percentage chance of scoring.

Controlling the boards Gaining the majority of the rebounds.

Cut A quick movement by an attacking player without the ball, but always ready to receive, to gain an advantage over the defence, usually directed towards the basket.

Cutter A player who cuts (see above) or breaks (see above).

Cutaway A player's move in

cutting for the basket after setting a screen (see below) situation.

'D' (i) An abbreviation of Defence. (ii) That part of the circle of the key outside the restricted area.

Dead Attacking players who have used their dribble.

Diamond and one A term used to describe a combination defence (see above) with four defenders playing a zone defence (see below) in a diamond formation (i.e. 1.2.1) with the fifth defender out chasing the ball or marking a particular opponent.

Dish out When a player penetrates (drives) inside and passes the ball to his team-mate.

Drill A repetitive practice.

Drive The movement of an attacking player dribbling towards the basket in an attempt to score.

Drop Step (i) A step backwards. (ii) A defensive movement in which a player executes a pivot backwards to stay with the opponent.

Double pick A screen when two offensive player stays together.

Double team When two defensive players mark one opponent with the ball, usually a temporary measure (see Trap).

Dunk A shot in which a jumping player puts the ball down into the opponent's basket from above.

Elbow The upper corner of the key area, where the sideline of the paint, the foul line and the circle of the key meet.

Fake A movement made with the aim of deceiving an opponent.

Fall away A method of performing certain shots and passes in which the player with the ball moves in one direction as the ball moves in another.

Fast break A fast attack that attempts to advance the ball to the front court before the defence is organized, with the object of achieving numerical superiority or a position to give a good shot.

Feed To pass the ball to a team-mate.

Flash If a player shows himself as open. This is combined with some quick steps towards the ball.

Floor play Used to describe the movements on the court of players of either team.

Fouled out Being required to leave the game after committing five fouls.

Foul line Free throw line.

Forward The name of one of the positions in the team. Forwards play on the sides of the court when their team is attacking either on the right or left hand side, between the restricted area (see below) and the sidelines.

Free ball (loose ball) A ball that, although in play, is not in the possession of either team.

Freelance An unstructured type of attack where players take advantage of whatever attacking opportunities arise.

Freezing the ball The action of the team in possession of the ball who try to retain possession without attempting to score. Limited to 24 seconds and often used late in the game in an effort to protect a slight lead.

Front court That half of the court that contains the basket that a team is attacking.

Fronting the post Guarding the post player (see below) in front, between the player and the ball, rather than between the player and the basket.

Front screen A screen set up by an attacking player between a team-mate and this team-mate's opponent.

Full court press A pressing defence, which is operated throughout the whole court and not merely in the defender's backcourt (see above).

Fundamentals The basic skills of the game, necessary as a background for all individual and team play.

Gap In a zone defence, gap refers to the area of the court where the zones of responsibility of two individual defenders meet. Also called a seam.

Give and go An attacking manoeuvre in which a player passes the ball to a team-mate and cuts (q.v.) towards the basket for a return pass.

Guard (playmaker/quarterback) The name of one of the positions on the team, usually played by the shorter players, who on attack will normally play in the area of court between the centre line and the free throw line extended to the side-lines.

Half court press A pressing defence, which operates in the team's backcourt.

Held ball Is 'declared when two players of opposing teams have one or both hands firmly on the ball'. See 'Rules'.

Help side The side of the defensive formation away from the ball, the weak side (see below). A defender on the help side will move to the ball to give depth to the defence and in particular be prepared to help the team-mate marking the ball handler.

High A position played by an attacking player near to the free throw line.

Hustle A characteristic of a player who plays hard at all time, especially when on defence. A player who pressures the opponent.

In-line The basic man-to-man defensive position 'in line' between the opponent and the basket being defended.

Inside (i) In and close to the restricted area. (ii) Between the perimeter of the defence and the basket they are defending.

In and out play When an outside player guard or forward passes the ball inside to the pivot and he passes it back (out) to the backcourt.

Jump stop A stop with the ball when the player takes and lands on both feet simultaneously.

Key (keyhole) The restricted area (see below) including the circle, derived from the original keyhole shape.

'L' cut A change of direction by an attacking player to evade a defender, usually made at right angles to the original direction.

Lane See 'Restricted area'.

Lead pass A pass thrown ahead of the intended receiver so that they can catch the ball on the move and maintain their speed.

Low A position held by an attacking player near to the end line.

Man-to-man defence (one to one defence) A style of defence where each player is assigned to guard a specific opponent, regardless of where they go in the attack.

Money Players often call a successful long-range or penalty shot 'money' after the 'slot machine' sound when winner hears the sound of falling coins.

Motion offence A style of attacking play with no predetermined order of movement of players or the ball. The attack is based upon constant movement of all five players. Players look to use basic individual and team plays to take advantage of defensive errors. Some order may be given to the movements by the coach introducing rules of action, for example every time a pass is made the passer looks to cut to the basket or set a screen away from the ball.

Nice touch A player who has excellent soft shot release.

Out-of-bounds The area outside the legal playing court, i.e. on or outside the boundary lines of the court.

Offence Attack.

Off Guard The guard (see above) who is a good passer and one of the best scorers on the team with longer-range shots.

Off-line A variation of 'in-line' defence (see above) in which the defender takes up a position slightly to one side of their opponents, but still between the opponent and the basket. The aim is to reduce the opponent's attacking options.

Off side (guard, forward, post) The player on the opposite side of the court to the side on which the ball is being played (see also weak side).

One on one (1 versus 1) The situation where one attacking player attacks one defensive player.

One to one defence A style of defence where each player is assigned to guard a specific opponent regardless of where they go in their attacking manoeuvres.

Options Alternative attacking manoeuvres that can occur in a game situation.

Outlet pass The first pass made after a defensive rebound (see below), usually made to initiate a fast break (see above).

Outside (i) Outside the restricted area. (ii) Between the sideline and perimeter of the defence.

Overload Outnumbering the defence.

Overplay When a defender positions himself on the ball side of the offence.

Overtime The extra period(s) played after the expiration of the second half of a game in which the score has been tied. Play is continued for an extra period of five minutes as for as many such periods of five minutes as may be necessary to break the tie.

Paint, 3-second area, restricted area An area under the basket where offensive players may stay only for the duration of three seconds. It is often painted a different colour to the rest of the court.

Pass and Cut See 'Give and go'

Pattern The predetermined positional formation adopted by an attacking team prior to initiating attacking manoeuvres. Common patterns are 1.3.1, 2.1.2 and 2.3.

Pattern play Attacking plays initiated from fixed and predetermined court positions.

Pick (side screen) A screen (see below) set at the side of a teammate's opponent.

Passing Game A motion offence (see above) with the emphasis on passing the ball with little or no use of the dribble.

Penetration Powerful dribble (drive) to the basket, which leaves individual or team defence behind.

Pick and roll A side screen followed by a pivot towards the basket by the player who has set the screen, useful against a switching man-to-man defence.

Pivot (i) 'A pivot takes place

when a player who, holding the ball, steps once or more than once in any direction with the same foot, the other foot called the pivot foot being kept at its point of contact with the floor.' See 'Rules'. (ii) Another name for a Post Player (see below).

Play maker A player who is adept at setting up situations that enable team-mates to have scoring opportunities (see also Guard).

Play A term used to describe a series of movements of players and/or the ball on court, mainly used for attacking manoeuvres.

Point guard The guard (see above) who takes the main responsibility for bringing the ball up court and controlling the attack.

Post (i) See 'Post player'. (ii) Attacking play in which a player takes up a position usually with their back to the basket they are attacking, thus providing a target to receive a pass.

Post player Usually the tallest player in the team, who operates on attack in an area near the sides of, and occasionally in, the free throw lane and close to the basket. They are stationed there for scoring purposes and to feed cutters (see above) and are players around whom the attacking team pivot. This player is therefore sometimes called a pivot player.

Press A defensive attempt to force the opposing team into making some kind of error and thus losing possession of the ball. It is accomplished usually by aggressive defence, double teaming (see above) or harassing the ball handler with attempts to tie-up (see below) the ball. The press can be applied full court, half court or any other fractional part of the playing area, and can be based on either man-to-man or zone (see below) principles.

Quarterback See 'Playmaker' or 'Guard'.

Rebound A term used to describe the actual retrieving of the ball as it rebounds from the backboard or the ring after an unsuccessful shot.

Rebound triangle A term used to describe the positioning of a group of three defenders who form a tri-angle around the basket after a shot has been attempted. The aim is to cover the probable positions of the ball should a rebound occur, and prevent an opponent from gaining a good position from which to collect the rebound.

Restraining circle The circles of 3.6m (12ft) diameter located in the centre of the court and at the free throw lines.

Restricted areas 'The restricted areas shall be spaces marked in the court which are limited by the end lines, the free throw lines and by lines, which originate at the end lines, their outer edges being 3m from the midpoint of the end lines and terminate at the end of the free throw lines.' See 'Rules'.

Reverse (i) A change of direction in the flow of attacking movement, for example a change from passing down the right-hand side of the court to a quick movement of the ball to the left side. (ii) A change of direction in which attacking players endeavour to free themselves from a close marking defender. The change of direction is executed after a move towards the defender and a pivot so that the attacking player turns their back on their opponent and then moves off in the new direction. Also called a roll or spin move.

Role player When a player's actions on the court are limited.

Run and gun When a team does not play organized basketball,

just runs back and forth and the first player who receives the ball takes a shot on the frontcourt. Very popular style of play in the English Premier Divison.

Safety man An attacking player who plays in the guard position with the aim of defending against possible fast breaks or loss of possession, and to receive a pass when an attacking play breaks down.

Sag When a defender moves away from their opponent towards the basket they are defending.

Sagging defence A team defensive tactic in which the defenders away from the ball sag off their opponents towards the basket to help their team-mates and cover the high percentage scoring area.

Screen A screen occurs when an attacking player attempts to prevent a defender from reaching a desired position or maintaining their defensive position. The screen is intended to impede the progress of the defender so that the attacking player they are marking has an unimpeded shot or a clear path to basket.

Screen and roll A side screen followed by a pivot towards the basket by the player who has set the screen, used against a switching man-to-man defence.

Scrimmage A practice game.

Seam See 'Gap'.

Set play (i) A repetitive, pre-arranged form of attack. (ii) A play (see above) executed to pre-determined and rehearsed moves which, when applied at certain set situations in the game, is intended to result in a favourable scoring chance. The set situations are usually out-of-bounds, jump ball or the free-throw situation.

Set-up The action of establishing an attacking pattern (see above) or the defensive organization.

141

GLOSSARY

Series A name given to a number of plays used by an attacking team in particular situations, for example high post plays.

Side screen A screen (see above) set at the side of a teammate's opponent.

Skip pass A pass made in an attack that misses out one or two players in the attacking formation.

Slow break A deliberate attack against a defence that is set-up (see above).

Splitting the post This occurs when two attacking players cross in front of a post player, cutting on opposite sides of the post player to the basket, in an attempt to lose their defenders on the post player.

Square up Face the basket, normally after receiving the ball.

Stack A situation where two or more attacking players stand close together very near to the restricted area (see above), usually in a low (see above) position.

Stall See 'Freezing the ball'.

Steal To take the ball from an opponent or intercept a pass.

Stride stop A stop with the ball performed using a 1–2 rhythm. The ball is received with both feet off the floor, one foot touches the floor, and then the trailing foot strides forward and lands to execute the stop.

Strong side This refers to the side of the court on which the attacking team has the ball. It can also refer to the side of the court on which the attacking team has the largest number of players.

Switch A defensive manoeuvre in which two defenders exchange defensive responsibilities by changing the player they are guarding. It occurs usually during a screen situation in which one of the defenders can no longer guard their opponent because of the screen.

System A team's basic attacking and defensive play.

Tie-up A defensive situation in which the defenders gain a held ball situation (see above) through their defensive tactics.

Tip The momentary catching and pushing of the ball whilst the player is in the air.

Tip-off The centre jump ball at the start of play.

Trailer An attacking player who follows behind the ball-handler.

Transition This occurs after the change of possession as a team moves from an attack to defence, and vice versa.

Trap A double team (see above) in which two defenders attempt to stop a dribbler and prevent that player making a successful pass. If successful, this could lead to an interception or five seconds' violation by the ball handler.

Triple Threat A position in which, with the ball at chest height, a player can shoot, pass or dribble.

Travelling When a player steps more than two while in possession of the ball, or commits stop or start violation.

Turnover The loss of ball possession without a shot being taken.

Turnaround jumper An athletic shot in which the shooter starts the shoot with their back to the basket and completes a 180-degree turn in mid-air before the ball is released.

'V' Cut A manoeuvre used by an attacking player to get free to receive a pass. The player without the ball makes a movement towards the basket and then cuts sharply at a 'V' angle towards the passer.

Weak side The opposite side of the court to the strong side (see above), that is, away from the ball.

Wing A term used to denote a position on court where the player is stationed between the end of the free throw line and the sideline.

Zone Defence A team's defensive tactic in which the five defensive players protect an area surrounding their basket within normal shooting range.

Index

INDEX